Women Saying No

Luath Press is an independently owned and managed book publishing company based in Scotland, and is not aligned to any political party or grouping. *Viewpoints* is an occasional series exploring issues of current and future relevance.

Women Saying No

Making a Positive Case
Against Independence

Edited By
MARIA FYFE

Luath Press Limited
EDINBURGH
www.luath.co.uk

First published 2014

ISBN: 978-1-910021-61-3

The paper used in this book is recyclable. It is made from
low chlorine pulps produced in a low energy, low emissions manner
from renewable forests.

Printed and bound by
Bell & Bain Ltd., Glasgow

Typeset in 11 point Sabon
by 3btype.com

All royalties from the sale of this book will go to the
Remember Mary Barbour fund.

My thanks to all those who have
expressed why they were voting NO.
They were asked to give it laldy.
They did.

Contents

Why We Are Voting NO

MARIA FYFE

I ONCE HAD A workmate who jumped over a wall, assuming that on the other side it was level with where he started. He had thought he was taking a shortcut, but it turned into a trip to the A&E. It could have been a bed of roses on the other side, or a bed of nettles. It was neither – it was the deep drop that put him in plaster. And it could have been much worse, as he ruefully admitted on his return to work.

If a majority of people living in Scotland decide to vote YES on 18 September 2014, then divorce from the rest of the UK will be easy to do. Easier than jumping over a wall. No expensive lawyers. No cost except the bus fare or the wear and tear on your shoes as you walk to the polling station. All the responsibility of bargaining over the share-out of the goods and the debts amassed over the years will lie with others. No need to lift a finger. You can leap into the unknown without even bothering to seek information. Just put a cross on a ballot paper. But the thing is, we are not voting in a General Election, when the outcome has a five-year span. This vote has consequences that could last for centuries to come. Divorcees have occasionally been known to change their minds and get back together again. But on the biggest question that has faced us these past 300 years, there is little or no prospect of getting back together. The Braveheartish sort of Nationalists will no doubt say 'that's fine by us, we would never want to do that.' Others will not want to burn bridges if they can avoid it. They also see our problems as ones we can solve together, rather than by extracting ourselves from the rest of the UK.

Think forward a few decades or even centuries. Why would people in England, Wales and Northern Ireland be in any hurry to let us rejoin a family of nations that we had walked out on, just when all four nations were still striving to recover from the world's worst recession in many decades? When wages were stagnant or reduced, people in work needed top-up benefits, food banks had grown to numbers never before imagined, housing was scarce and grossly over-priced, young people were without prospects of decently paid work, and our NHS was struggling? All this affecting every nation in the UK, but we had decided to go it alone, instead of working together. And on top of that, if Alex Salmond had his way, we had cut corporation tax with the intention of taking jobs and investment away from England.

On the other hand, if we vote NO, we allow ourselves endless possibilities for how things could change for the better, for all of us in the UK. I say could, not will, because just putting a cross on a ballot paper is not enough. It never has been.

It is simply not true that we will be lumped with the status quo. No political party is offering that. Look at the evidence. The SNP keep harking back to 1979 when the UK Parliament did not deliver devolution. They never mention 1997, when it did, John Smith having declared it 'the settled will of the Scottish people.'

The very existence of the Scottish Parliament proves the UK Parliament can be persuaded that change is necessary and deliver it. So why would anyone believe that their best option is to jump over a wall and hope for the best? A&E departments deal with this kind of thing every day of the week, but no one is suggesting that's a good idea.

Ah, but I hear women voting YES say that they do want divorce from the people who brought us the Poll Tax, the bedroom tax, lower taxes for the rich, Trident and unwanted wars.

So here are just a few reminders. The poll tax was brought to us by Scottish Tories. It was they who persuaded Margaret Thatcher, it was not imposed on us by England. The bedroom tax will be repealed if Labour is elected in 2015 – no more need for the Scottish Parliament to compensate victims of this vile policy. Lower taxes for the rich? It is Alex Salmond who promises to cut corporation tax lower than even George Osborne plans to do.

Trident? Not quite the wholehearted commitment to get rid of it that the Nationalists have built so much support on. Read the words in the White Paper and guess how long it will be for Trident to actually go. But there is commitment to NATO, and permission for all its member states' vessels to visit Scottish ports whether carrying nuclear weapons or not.

There is even a declaration from Alex Salmond that the USA could have bases in Scotland. Doing what, precisely, has not yet been revealed.

Wars? We have only recently seen the UK Parliament respond to public opinion and vote against military action in Syria. Attitudes have shifted since Iraq.

Supporters of left-wing pro-independence parties are, of course, republican to the core. So were the Scottish Nationalists in days of old when they used to sing, to the tune of 'The Sash My Father Wore':

Oh Scotland hasnae got a king, and she hasnae got a queen.
How can there be a saicint Liz when the first yin's never been?
Nae Liz the wan, nae Lillibet the twa, nae Liz will ever dae,
For we'll mak' oor land republican in a Scottish breakaway.

But to gain a republic enough people will have to be persuaded to vote for parties that advocate it. It may be unkind, but nevertheless true, to point out the minimal success of the Greens. Not one candidate representing any of the ultra-left parties has been elected to the Scottish Parliament, or the UK Parliament, since the downfall of Tommy Sheridan. Many a deposit has been lost. However, I have to congratulate them on their ingenuity in solving the problem of how to advance their cause without exposing their huge differences with the SNP, their mates in the YES campaign, in terms of what they think an independent Scotland should deliver. For the past two years, they have got away with telling groups of like-minded people that they were not nationalists, and thereby avoided having to answer criticisms of the SNP. So convenient to ignore the fact that a YES vote would put the party whose whole reason for existence has now been won, not themselves, well ahead in the following election. And so convenient for the SNP to let their stooges paint a picture that would never be a reality if they were in power.

They carefully avoided open splits with the SNP until as late as June 2014 – three months before the referendum – when they had no choice. What else could they do when the SNP reiterated their intention of keeping the monarchy, and putting this into their draft Constitution?

Other left wingers with republican views but who are committed to voting NO recognise the reality that more work has to be done to achieve widespread agreement that bringing an end to a monarchy that sits at the pinnacle of the class system would be a Good Thing.

It's been noted over and over again that women are more likely to vote NO than YES. There has been endless speculation about why, but little expression of their views has been heard. It has to be noted that some of those who were asked to set out their thoughts for this collection of essays told me they felt they couldn't. A few working in fields funded by the Scottish Government felt it would be risky. Some felt physically frightened. They had been shouted at by men unknown to them, telling them to go and live in England if they liked it so much. Others with English accents, when overheard chatting with their mates in a pub, were told to 'get back to England.' That is one end of the spectrum, and bad enough. At the other end, one particular individual received death threats at the time of the last referendum, required police protection, and finally had to move house. There have been public meetings where Better Together speakers have been shouted down, unable to be heard. In June 2014 we had the spectacle of the First Minister's Special Advisor – paid by the public's taxes – attacking Clare Lally, a young mother of a severely disabled child, who dared to speak publicly in support of a NO vote, immediately joined by cybernats delivering childish insults and abuse. This is a worrying aspect of the referendum campaign that is now getting the exposure it deserves. Is this the kind of Scotland we want to live in?

But here and now we have a collection of essays by women who do speak out clearly and firmly in support of a NO vote. They vary in age, ethnicity, political views and life experiences. They have varying reasons for their decision. Women do not all think the same thoughts, which seems to come as a surprise to some commentators. I thank Luath Press for making this publication possible.

Constitutional Change
is not Enough

JOHANN LAMONT MSP

WHY AM I VOTING NO in the referendum? An interesting question, and one that people across Scotland are contemplating ahead of 18 September.

My decision to vote NO is a positive vote for the politics of co-operation and the politics of change. I am voting NO because I am a proud Scot, not despite it. I am voting NO because I am a socialist and a feminist; I am voting NO because I believe profoundly that the things that drive my politics – the determination to tackle inequality and injustice, to create a fairer world, to ensure our young people can achieve their full potential, to make sure we have dignity in our old age – all of my aspirations for our communities can be better achieved in the UK.

The UK allows us to share and pool resources and risk, redistributing wealth from the richer parts of the country to the poor; it helps us manage economic shocks and uneven economic growth in different parts of the country.

Brought up in inner-city Glasgow, I saw children denied the opportunity to learn and thrive; I saw people who worked hard but whose efforts were poorly rewarded. Every summer I headed for the Isle of Tiree, where people worked just as hard on land they did not own and where the memories of the struggles of the land leaguers against the landowners were still fresh. I learned then that exploitation takes many forms and that the challenge is to confront that exploitation, not to view that exploitation differently, depending on the nationality of the exploiter or the exploited.

Being Scottish did not make the factory owner less resistant to the campaigns to give working people basic rights and being Scottish certainly did not inhibit landowners from clearing people from the land they worked.

Like most Scots, I see the common sense argument that sharing resources for pensions and health across 60 million people is better than across six million.

I know that we as Scots benefit from the UK, but it is clear too that we see the fairness in contributing to the UK as well, whether it is our natural assets, our talents or our creativity. I love that Scots look outwards, are open to new ideas, and confident enough in themselves not to be threatened by co-operating with others.

But there is a bigger question and that is about the purpose of politics and how you create change.

Too often the constitutional debate has become the politics of grievance, that all the ills visited upon us are caused by others – by the rest of the UK. And rather than a Scottish Parliament that uses its powers to make a difference, to show what we can do, we have Scottish Government Minister after Scottish Government Minister telling us what we cannot do, settling for alibi rather than action: using the Parliament as a platform for separation, rather than a forum for developing the measures to improve lives.

That is a politics that is corrosive and a politics in which those who need power to be exercised in their interests most, suffer most.

Where politics should be about choices, often choices amongst many different good things, we see in this debate a constitutional offer where everyone can have what they want, where we can cut taxes and spend more, where everything is promised and nothing costed.

People sometimes say that the decision we face on 18 September is the biggest decision in 300 years. I don't think it is. I like to think that supporting universal compulsory education, the NHS, universal suffrage, abolishing slavery, protecting workers' rights, fighting for equality for women, tackling racism, uniting to fight Fascism – and so many more – were all decisions of far greater significance.

But if we collude with the idea that constitutional change is enough, that progressive values are inevitable if we only change the constitution, we deny a simple truth. To win change you have to win the political argument. You have to identify the causes of inequality and win the political case to tackle them.

I know that no step on the road to greater equality was ever easy or granted without a struggle. I want the people of Scotland to vote NO, to resist the easy offers and instead pledge to work with all those who hunger for change, for equality, for all those radical voices, whatever their nationality, willingly to take on the arguments, create the solutions and improve the future for all our children.

There are those who see this referendum as a test of our Scottishness. It is not.

This debate is not Scotland versus England or Scotland versus the Tories. It is an argument amongst Scots, a choice of two visions – one insular and turning away, the other open, embracing the interdependency of our world.

I want a strong, united Scotland, shaping the future of the UK. And at its heart I want a politics of ideas, of discourse, of action; an optimistic politics rooted in our soaring ambition for all to achieve their potential; a politics which will not settle for the swapping of slogans or false hope.

That is the opportunity that voting NO on 18 September offers. I, for one, shall grasp that opportunity with all my might.

JOHANN LAMONT is the Leader of the Scottish Labour Party, the first person to be elected to that role created in 2012. She has been the Scottish Labour and Co-operative MSP for Glasgow Pollok since the establishment of Scottish Parliament in 1999. She was Deputy Minister for Communities from October 2004 to November 2006 and Deputy Minister for Justice from November 2006 to May 2007. She was born in Glasgow in 1957 to a Gaelic-speaking family from Tiree. She is married to Archie Graham and has two children, Fay and Colin. She keeps fit by walking, jogging and dancing. Her political interests are tackling poverty, women's rights, rights of disabled people and others who experience discrimination. She supports Fair Trade. She attended Woodside Secondary School, Glasgow, then obtained MA Hons at University of Glasgow, the Postgraduate teaching qualification at Jordanhill College of Education and the Certificate of Guidance at University of Strathclyde. Prior to being elected, she worked as a class teacher for 20 years.

CHAPTER I

Why I'm Voting NO

SARAH BOYACK MSP

I AM VOTING NO because I believe that devolution gives us the best of both worlds, with a strong Scottish Parliament and direct representation at the UK level too.

I campaigned for devolution because I believed that decision making needed to be brought closer to home in Scotland. I wanted more accountability in the decisions taken in relation to health, education, transport, environment, our legal system and our economy. The Scottish Parliament gives us that accountability and gives us the chance to shape policies and laws to meet our needs.

We have much to gain from the solidarity that comes from working with the rest of the UK. We have strong family connections, a social partnership and shared economies with our English, Welsh and Northern Irish neighbours. Our family ties, friendships, institutions, businesses and ideas offer a strength that millions of us value across the UK. I don't want to lose those relationships.

In the modern world, I can't see that it makes any sense to separate our economy, which is integrated with the rest of the UK, to unpick our pensions, our welfare and our national insurance systems.

With all the problems we currently face, spending the next few years removing ourselves from the shared UK institutions that we helped create seems a huge distraction from the real world. Even worse, spending precious political and financial resources replicating those institutions or negotiating to be able to use them seems to me to be an almighty waste of energy.

We'd lose the benefits we have now with Scottish companies able to trade and invest across the UK. Our financial services gain from the single regulatory framework in the UK. Our renewables industry has been able to grow at a phenomenal rate, supported by a third of the UK's renewables investment because of the UK's integrated energy market. Our universities gain from the research and investment from UK research councils. And people are able to benefit from NHS facilities across the UK whether it's for specialist heart services or treatment for a tropical disease or to give birth to triplets.

There's a cost to leaving the UK and then wanting to use the pound. I've spent the last couple of decades hearing SNP representatives complain that our economy is driven from the city of London – yet the irony is they'd remove our representation from the UK Parliament, and remove our capacity to exert influence on the legislation which governs those financial institutions. If Scotland voted YES, it would not be automatic that we could continue to use the pound and it would not be on our terms.

It's also clear that, despite the assertions in the SNP Government's White Paper, we'd have to apply to be a member of the European Union. I'm less worried about whether we'd be allowed to join, but much more concerned about the terms on which we'd be a member and the possibility of a lengthy process. We'd lose the benefit of the opt outs the UK has negotiated. As a former Minister who's attended European meetings, I believe we get the best of both worlds in the EU. We get the benefit of being part of the UK team in Europe and we get to build relationships with other EU members where we've got shared interests. We need to develop those relationships rather than starting from scratch again.

We should instead be focusing on building on the success we've been able to achieve, benefitting from being part of the UK economy and continuing to develop industries such as our financial services, our energy and renewables and food and drinks industries.

We should be tackling the big challenges of our age – creating public services that meet our changing demographic needs, responding to global climate challenges and maximising our resources as one of the world's wealthiest countries to eradicate poverty and inequality both in our own communities and across the globe.

To all of those above challenges, independence is at best a distraction. At worst, it makes these challenges even harder.

It's now 15 years since the new Scottish Parliament was established. It's a measure of the success of devolution that it would be unthinkable to go back to the days before the Scottish Parliament existed. But there is scope for improvement in terms of how the Parliament works. We should use the debate on our constitutional future to strengthen our democratic structures and reflect on how we can make devolution meet our current priorities.

Change is already on the way. The 2012 Scotland Act brought more control on income tax, devolution of stamp duty and landfill tax and new borrowing powers to the tune of around £5 billion. The Better Together parties have all proposed new powers to strengthen devolution. Stronger devolution is a much better way forward than independence and all the uncertainty separation would bring.

Labour's proposals from our 'Devolution Commission: Powers for a Purpose' were the result of a year of debate and consultation. Our task was to consider how we could both strengthen the Scottish Parliament and retain the benefits of sharing our resources and working together across the UK. A key objective was to develop proposals to reverse the SNP's damaging centralisation agenda. Our vision for devolution was never that the Scottish Parliament should gain powers from the UK level, then remove powers from our local councils, centralising decision making and putting local government in a financial straightjacket, as the SNP have done.

For us, it's not a question of power for the sake of it but what powers we believe we need to create prosperity and a more equal society. We focused on devolving powers that would enable us to be more effective in creating jobs and getting people back into work. We therefore propose devolving the Work Programme to local authorities to enable them to work with the third sector to give people the support they need.

We also propose empowering local authorities to work with local employers and local colleges to provide training opportunities by abolishing Skills Development Scotland. We'd ensure that the Scottish Parliament could set national priorities on training but ensure that our local councils are able to generate the skills locally that are needed to create the strong local economies we need if we are to be successful.

Trade unions raised the need to strengthen enforcement of health and safety legislation. It makes sense to have the same health and safety regime across the UK, but we want to see a higher priority given to ensuring that we have safer workplaces with a clear lead given at the Scottish level and backed by action at the local level.

We'd keep our UK framework for equalities, but again would devolve enforcement and promotion of equalities to the Scottish Parliament. The same approach would apply to employment tribunals, where we propose to keep the UK legislative framework, but devolve the operation of tribunals. Our proposals are driven by a desire to increase equality and fairness in society generally and our workplaces in particular.

Our plans also mean that the next Labour Government will devolve housing benefit and enable the Scottish Parliament not just to abolish the hated bedroom tax, but also to build the affordable social housing, which is desperately needed. Again, we need to set priorities at the Scottish level but devolve power and financial resources to the local level to enable local councils to address local needs and to support local communities.

In reversing the SNP's centralisation agenda, we need not just to pass responsibility to local councils, but the capacity to act. The SNP have broken local government finance. We need debate across the political parties to develop long-term solutions to fund local government services.

The last year has seen several reports highlighting the need to reshape services to meet the demographic challenges we face, such as providing decent social care services and creating sustainable infrastructure for our communities. We've suggested as a starting point that local councils be given the option of using a tourist levy on non-UK taxpayers. There are also major opportunities that could be exploited from developing local community renewables projects, where councils benefit from the heat and power created and we can eradicate the scandal of fuel poverty that scars communities.

Our approach is double devolution – empowering our communities by transferring power to local councils and on to local communities. Our geography is varied and one size doesn't fit all when it comes to the shape of local services. The debate being promoted under the 'Our Islands Our Future' banner needs to be embraced.

One of the benefits of devolution is that it has let us learn from experience elsewhere and work together across the UK when it makes sense. There is much we could learn from the Co-operative Councils network across the UK and the City Deals agenda in England.

The long, drawn out independence debate comes at a cost. It's crowding out issues that we should be acting on now. Scotland is on pause.

While many organisations have quite rightly taken the chance to air their issues and concerns through the independence debate, it does mean that those issues are viewed through the prism of independence rather than in their own right.

There are also far too many issues that have been simply put on hold for the duration of the referendum campaign. In my view, it's been a cynical strategy to hold off on addressing issues where people need help and action now so that the UK Government can be blamed to build the case for separation. The SNP Government ignored our calls for a year to act on the bedroom tax. This meant local councils were not able to access much needed cash to help get tenants support.

There are other areas where more could be done now. The policy framework and action needed to eradicate fuel poverty by 2016 is not there. The Marine Scotland Act was passed in 2010, but we're still waiting for the Marine Plan which was meant to follow it to protect our marine environment. The rates at which the Land and Buildings Transaction Tax will be levied won't be announced until after the referendum. Action on childcare came only after huge pressure. Seven years of SNP Government and we're still waiting to hear the promised solutions for making local government funding fairer.

So I'll be voting NO in the referendum in September – but supporting increased powers for the Scottish Parliament. I believe it's the best of both worlds. Devolution means we can grow the Scottish economy as part of the UK.

Independence puts jobs at risk, especially in Edinburgh's finance and banking sector. The economic uncertainty simply isn't worth it, with the risks of higher interest rates and holding back the economic recovery in the new jobs we desperately need.

Pensions matter to everyone and people are understandably concerned about the unanswered pension questions that would come with independence. Scotland currently gets £200 million more for pensions than our population share of the UK would dictate. A better retirement for everyone is just one of the many benefits we gain from being part of the UK.

One of the successes of devolution has been the development of targeted relationships internationally. The Fresh Talent Initiative enabled young people to come to study and then contribute economically to Scotland. Our partnership with Malawi demonstrates the benefits of our work as a devolved nation alongside and complementing the UK's aid programme. We've also seen trade unions, schools, communities and faith groups join together to use our consumer power to make Scotland a Fair Trade Nation.

Solidarity on the global stage doesn't require independence. Being part of the UK hasn't stopped us playing our part in attending climate change conferences or developing progressive relationships with other countries using our trade and civic links to mutual benefit. Scotland as a devolved nation can have a greater influence working as part of the UK and in the EU than we would do alone.

SARAH BOYACK MSP is Labour's Shadow Cabinet Member for Local Government and Planning. She chairs the Cross Party Group on International Development and is Co-Convenor of the CPG on energy Efficiency and Renewables. She was first elected in 1999, having previously been a town planner in local government and Edinburgh College of Art/Heriot Watt University.

CHAPTER 2

I'll Admit It, I'm Feart

ESME CLARK

THIS IS ME. I'm not a pundit, a politician or (heaven help me) an account-ant. I'm a woman, not long retired, an Anglo-Scot living in Glasgow, happy to make my home here, and loving the lifestyle with a lot to look forward to in 2014. (I've been lucky enough to get tickets for the Games!)

I had a Scottish father and an English mother and, although I was born in England, I've lived in Scotland all my adult life. Most of the people I know have had an English relative, a Welsh grannie or a granddad who came over from Ireland at some point. We're a handsome people in the UK, the red-headed Celts and a few gloriously fair leftovers from the days of the Vikings, some genes left over from the Romans and all the different tribes that came to form the UK, as well as the new immigrants who have enriched our country. If we went through a supermarket-type scanner, it would be printed indelibly on our bottoms 'product of more than one country.'

This is a good time to be a woman living in the UK, with all the opportunities it offers. As we come out of the recession, opportunities are opening up for young people throughout the land, but you don't need to be in the first bloom of youth to appreciate what we have. I was down in London for the Jubilee, and felt the warm rush of belonging, of a sense of a shared history that has seen us through World Wars and economic upheavals, seen our banks falter and seen the might of a large economy take the strain of supporting them. I love London, but have had my own *Braveheart* moment when I've seen the massed pipes come over the hill (I appreciate them more in the open air, as I used to live next door to a keen piper who practised on a Sunday morning). The sound of a Welsh male voice choir is one of the most sublime in the musical world and a Northern colliery brass band from my mother's home village can bring me to the verge of tears.

Why would we want to take apart something that works? It could be done. The doomsayers that predict Scotland would end up in Dickensian-type poverty, begging for bread or a handout from the EU do the argument no favours. Of course we could separate, but if anyone thinks it would be easy, they are kidding themselves. We all know of divorces where the two parties involved ended up exhausted and bitterly regretting it, still arguing who gets custody of Fluffy while the only ones who are still smiling are the lawyers. This is after a few years of marriage – imagine what it would take to separate nations! The financial implications for banks, for the armed forces, for our pensions and taxes and the parcelling out of obligations for debts. We wouldn't have national teams anymore and our commercial heartland would suffer damage that would take decades to recover. I loved the old Ealing comedy *Passport to Pimlico* where that London borough makes a bid for independence. It is bemused to find that shopkeepers have to deal with the Export Department from their suppliers, and the crime rate soars. Finally it decides to come back to join the rest of us. An independent Scotland would have to fight for its markets. England, Wales and Northern Ireland take a vast amount of our goods. Would they always? I don't know, and it worries me. The big supermarkets would have to think how they would operate in an independent Scotland, under a different tax system. As would the large companies who have their Scottish offices in Edinburgh, Glasgow or Aberdeen, or the companies who are investing in the new technologies in Dundee, creating a serious number of jobs.

I'll admit it, I'm feart. I have paid my pension contributions to the UK pension scheme and my personal pension comes from an English-based company. I know I wouldn't be left penniless, there would be some adjustments to be made, and eventually I would be sorted out, but when you are older, you don't have the years left to wait until it is all resolved and I get something like what I'm used to. Basically, I suppose I don't trust an SNP independent government to deliver its promises, however good their intentions. They can't offer cast-iron guarantees because this would be a totally new situation. With the best will in the world, they can't tell how it would go. Would the EU take us in on the same terms as the rest of the UK or would we have to apply as a new nation? Keep the pound? Then would we have to work with the Bank of England on the bank rate? What about the monarchy? Different taxes could mean some checks having to be made, some borders having to be put in place to avoid smuggling. *Passport to Pimlico* could become *Passport to Berwick*, more like.

Always one to see the absurdities in life, it does occur to me that there's something I haven't heard being discussed. What would happen to our national collections? The British Museum and all the Galleries throughout the UK, with their international reputations? After all, they were partially funded by the taxpayers of Scotland and there have been many generous benefactors of Scottish descent. Could there be a sort of supermarket sweep when the Scots curators descend on the galleries – 'We'll have a Rubens, a little Rembrandt and a few Picassos, please.' We could even end up with our own wee Elgin Marble, for all the good it might do us. If the National Theatre goes, we could end up with a time-share in Dame Helen Mirren.

When the vote comes, I hope people vote for the right reasons, and have thought it through. I worry that the electorate for this vote includes those who will not be hanging around to see what happens and excludes those thousands of Scots who have an interest in the vote, but who are living and working temporarily in other parts of the UK. That's right – the thousands of Scots who are living and working in other parts of the UK but who consider themselves Scottish and care deeply what happens to this nation.

I don't want to have to decide whether I'm Scottish or English. I don't want my relatives living in England to be strangers in a foreign country. I'm proud of my Scottish heritage – I feel Scottish when I'm home here and British when I go down South or when I'm travelling abroad. My British passport is important to me, and I feel safer being part of such a country. I feel we benefit socially, as well as economically and culturally by being part of the UK. We shouldn't put up barriers to opportunity that could hurt our young people.

One of my Christmas presents was a small ceramic plate. It reads 'Friends are the Family you Choose for Yourself.' I have chosen Scotland – I wasn't born here, but this is my home. Moving on into the 21st century, I truly believe that we are Better Together.

ESME CLARK is an Anglo-Scot, a retired bookseller, who now lives in Govan, Glasgow, an area which still retains a strong sense of community and an appreciation of its rich historical past. She has been seen dancing down the Royal Mile at Festival time, following those pipes and drummers, and when she was in London at the time of the Jubilee, she waved a Union Jack with great enthusiasm. She enjoys being Scottish and being English, and is happy to call herself British in any census.

CHAPTER 3

The Biggest Decision

PAM DUNCAN-GLANCY

THE DEBATE WE are having on Scotland's future will be the biggest decision we've made as a country for generations. Everyone must have their say, but crucially, the seldom heard in our communities – women, disabled people, LGBT people, BME people and so on – must have theirs. And that's what our unions, activists and charities, working in and for our communities, do best – make Scotland a better place to live. They are the voices of the voiceless.

I am a disabled woman. I grew up in the North of Scotland, I live in Glasgow now, my mum was from London and my dad from Glasgow. I have been an equalities and human rights activist for as a long as I can remember. Without the support of our unions, charities and activists for social justice, I wouldn't have a home, a job, a husband or even a life. That's why I'm voting NO in 2014 – no to separation, no to destabilising our unions and charities and no to splitting us from our closest and strongest comrades – the activists for social justice and equality, the length and breadth of the United Kingdom.

Our unions and charities have been at the forefront of supporting social justice, equality and human rights activism for decades, seeking to change things for the people they represent – across communities, across characteristics and across borders.

Now, as we slide into deeper and deeper financial difficulty, is not the time to de-stabilise our unions, charities and our activism – and the lives of those they represent. Now is not the time to divide, but come together.

On a really basic level, the potential transition and overhead costs of any change could cripple our unions and charities. Not to mention the fact that 48 per cent of people say they'd be less likely to give to charities if they only operated in Scotland. As part of the UK, a bigger country, we can pool our resources and spread the risks we face across the broader shoulders of the United Kingdom – and that's what we do.

But more importantly, we gain strength in numbers, not just fiscally, but ideologically.

Within the disability sector we learn from our colleagues across the UK, sometimes from their mistakes but often from their successes – and we also share our resources. For too long, unions and the third sector have been treated as just that, third in line in the debate and third in line for the resources. That's why our links across the broader shoulders of the UK are crucial – cutting our unions and charities up could only cut these links, not build on them – we need them and they need us, together.

That's why I am voting NO in 2014. Not because I don't believe we can go it alone, but because I don't believe in dividing us. Together we are stronger, divided we are weak, divided we are ruled – not by our members, but by our funders. Our people need us, they need us strong and unshaken. And we need them, every single one of them, in Moray, Motherwell, Madeley and Middlesbrough.

PAM DUNCAN-GLANCY is Policy Officer for a national disabled people's organisation. She has a MSc in Health Psychology, a BSc in Psychology and a PGCert in Citizenship and Human Rights. Pam has been a disability activist for many years, is a keen trade unionist and a member of Scottish Labour's Social Justice Sounding Board. She served as Disabled Students Officer for NUS Scotland for two years and was also previously an Independent Living Adviser at Glasgow Centre for Inclusive Living. Pam has also been a board member of a national charity.

CHAPTER 4

Of Course It Couldn't Happen Here... Or Could It?

ANNA DYER

REMEMBER ALEX SALMOND'S 'arc of prosperity' of Ireland, Iceland and Norway that he urged we should join? As a woman, I always felt sceptical about that. How many of us would have liked to live in Ireland this past century, where women only make up less than 16 per cent of their Parliament, ranking 87th in the world and way down the table with both Koreas? The fight for Irish freedom didn't do much for women. Or Iceland, where enough women felt so let down, they formed a political party of their own that has won a few seats. As for Norway, it was not independence from Sweden that delivered its social democratic achievements. In that regard, its record is pretty similar.

Looking at the list of countries given by Salmond that have held a referendum since 1960 there are two categories – countries which have been decolonised since 1945 and the states of the former USSR and Eastern Europe. The record of the latter states is not scrutinised by the SNP. Yet the issues, which have arisen as a result of becoming independent, do in fact have great relevance to the referendum debate – it's just that the outcomes of their development don't help the Nationalist case.

I will be voting NO in the referendum based upon my experience of working and living in the new independent states of Eastern Europe. I have been a manager of large civil society and economic regeneration projects in Russia and Eastern Europe since 1990. In 2003 I became Director of a large project to establish a network of Women's Employment and Information Centres in Lithuania. This was part of a large programme to promote women's employment and rights throughout the new states. You may wonder why such projects were necessary, 13 years after the establishment of the new countries. When we look at what has happened to the position of women in these countries, it becomes obvious.

Before the break-up of the Soviet economic bloc in 1989 the situation was quite different. The percentage of women participating in political, public and economic life was even greater than in many EU countries.

In the national legislative bodies, the percentage of women members was 25 per cent to 33 per cent before 1989 with only the odd exception, and in local government it was even greater. Women's participation at all political levels was protected in almost all states by a quota system guaranteed by law. The immediate effect of the transition to independence was a drastic decline in the number of women MPs. Today the Russian Federation is 13.6 per cent (having risen from a low of five per cent in 1990) with Romania, Georgia, Ukraine and Hungary even less. Coupled with the impact of the economic changes, women became invisible.

But surely the situation got better as prosperity improved?

Well, by the end of the '90s the answer was 'not much' in politics or the economy. Hence the drive of the EU to support projects for the advancement of women.

So what is the position now?

Unfortunately, aid projects cannot make a revolutionary change, though they can in the long-term help to improve the situation and make a real difference. There has been progress in some countries. If we take the ten East European EU member states, the lower chambers of the Parliaments of Bulgaria, Czech Republic, Estonia, Latvia and Poland have from 20 to 22 per cent women members, but with Lithuania scoring 17 per cent followed by Romania, Slovenia and Slovakia, we reach the bottom with Hungary at 8.8 per cent. So why have women disappeared from public life?

The external drivers in the process of transition were the preachers of free market economics and rampant monetarism supported by the tantalising promises of foreign investment and friendly media coverage. It was not surprising that across Eastern Europe the dominant parties that emerged had a centre-right orientation. Proportional representation systems spawned a plethora of factions and parties, which meant that governments were formed from negotiations in smoky committee rooms dominated, of course, by male leaders. Women were not considered important so quotas were abolished and women disappeared from the candidate lists.

In almost every country, women constituted 50 per cent of the labour force before 1989. They occupied the middle levels of management and supervision in many state enterprises and many were technical experts, scientists and engineers. With the privatisation of state enterprises and the closing down of traditional industries the majority became unemployed. The pro-market ideology dominating these governments led to low corporation taxes (ten per cent in Bulgaria, for instance) in an attempt to attract foreign investment. Savage cuts in state budgets resulted in massive redundancies in ministries whose middle management levels were largely occupied by women. The slashing of budgets led to cuts in education, health and social services, 60 per cent of whose professionals were women. The liberal-democratic regimes would naturally stress entrepreneurship as the solution to the problems created by the economic collapse, backed by their policies, but women were refused credits and excluded from the male networks and connections so vital to creating a prosperous new business.

To make matters worse, with the cuts came the collapse of the network of free childcare services, which had been provided by state facilities and by the state enterprises. Expensive privatised childcare replaced them. Under the new regimes, maternity rights diminished or were simply non-existent, increasing unemployment further.

Women had to survive through part-time work and often several low-paid simultaneous jobs as unemployment benefit, if it existed at all, was derisory. Many of the younger unemployed left for work in other countries, but for women with children this was usually not an option. An important task of the EU Women's Projects was addressing the issue of trafficking, as many young, often well educated women were lured abroad to apparently safe and respectable jobs. At home finding employment increasingly favoured the young, good-looking and well educated. Older women had little chance of finding a job.

The disappearance of women from both political and economic life led to the domestication of women and made it easier for governments to permit the continued erosion of women's rights. It is notable that the lowest number of women MPs was in Hungary, which was hailed as a success story in attracting foreign investment by Western economists and politicians. It was however dominated by right-wing parties and the strongest nationalist politics of the East European states. The only jobs we heard of women getting were pole dancing.

The 'domestication' reinforced with nationalism and theocracy in some countries led to increasing restrictions on abortion rights and family planning. Poland for instance has some of Europe's strongest restrictions on abortion, the Catholic Church at the fore of campaigning for this legis-lation. Even where the toughest conditions are met, doctors frequently refuse to carry out procedures, leaving women to resort to illegal and highly dangerous do-it-yourself or backstreet abortions. Many doctors also refuse to give prescriptions for contraceptives.

Opinion polls conducted among East European women have demon-strated that while many young, well-educated women see opportunities in the future and think that life is better than before 1989, the vast majority of women over 35 years old think they are financially and socially worse off than before.

The lack of female representatives in the political system has made women create their own organisations and use other channels to campaign for their interests. There are many Non-Governmental Organisations fighting for women's rights and advancement and there has been some progress. I had the pleasure of working with many very strong, warm and capable women in Eastern Europe and many of them have remained good friends over the years. I take great pleasure in their achievements and the progress of the organisations that have fought so hard for survival. Political studies show that the representation of women in social demo-cratic parties is much better and some of them have voluntarily intro-duced quotas for selection of female candidates. This is reflected in the much higher proportion of women MEPs since these parties have gained more seats in the European Parliament. Of the ten East European states, 35.4 per cent of the MEPs from the social democratic parties in 2009 were women. Right-wing parties, by contrast, are mainly Euro-sceptic and of course have fewer women MEPs among their much smaller numbers.

So what lessons for women can be derived from the experience of Eastern Europe?

The hard-fought rights and achievements which women in Scotland, along with their sisters elsewhere in the UK, have struggled for over so many years can be very fragile, particularly in time of economic and political instability. And before any Scottish Nationalist claims Scotland wouldn't be like that, let's look at a few facts. Their own women MSPs, as a percentage of the SNP group in the Scottish Parliament, has fallen drastically from 43 per cent in 1999 to 26 per cent today. Yet their manifesto, otherwise known as the guide to an independent Scotland, makes no commitment to remedying that. If everything is going to be fairer in an independent Scotland, why is there no commitment to equal pay in the White Paper? The SNP Government has presided over 80,000 fewer women on part-time courses in further education since they came to office. They want more women in work, but they won't fund the courses that enable women, whose family circumstances prevent them from going full-time, to improve their chances. As for promises for childcare, we are told that we can't have a fuller programme now, because the income taxes paid would go to the UK Treasury. By that logic, Alex Salmond should cease going on missions abroad to bring jobs to Scotland, because every penny of new Income Tax paid would likewise 'go into George Osborne's back pocket.'

Their latest eye-catching policy is to insist on women forming 40 per cent of large company boards. Just like in Norway. This shows their inexperience in such matters. In Norway, so often held up to us for admiration, companies have got round the law by appointing women who have little or no say, but are there to make up the numbers. The real glass ceiling, which they would tackle if they were serious, is the pay and prospects of female workers in these enterprises, by enforcing audits to compare male with female employees.

If any woman imagines voting YES is the answer, achieved just by putting a cross on a ballot paper, she should look at the experience of women in other European countries where the rhetoric before independence turned out not to match the outcome. They were promised the earth, but bit the dust. Be assured, if Scotland votes YES, we will still need women's organisations to defend everything that has been achieved, never mind gain any improvements.

The biggest threat is a toxic mix of right-wing economics (cleverly hidden behind social-democratic patter) and nationalism, which embodies a populism with a lack of real political values. We cannot take it for granted that independence would bring to Scotland the promised land of prosperity, freedom and a golden future for all. That's what women in Eastern Europe thought.

ANNA DYER is a well-known community activist in Glasgow and is currently Chair of one of Scotland's largest community organisations. She is also at present Chair of Glasgow Labour Women's Forum. Originally an academic specialist in Soviet Studies, she worked as a researcher at the Semasko Institute of Public Health in Moscow. Her wide career experience included managing commercial projects and also economic regeneration and civil society projects in Eastern Europe and the former Soviet Union for the UK Government and EC.

CHAPTER 5

Why a NO Vote is Best for Women

MARIA FYFE

AS A WOMAN I find numerous reasons to be wary of the outcome of a YES vote. In January this year we found out something of importance to women, that had been kept under wraps, through a Parliamentary question tabled by Mary Scanlon MSP, Conservative education spokeswoman. It was revealed that 80,000 fewer women were studying part-time in Scotland's further education colleges since the SNP came to power. In 2007–08 there were nearly 182,000 women studying on part-time courses at college, but that fell to 101,000 last year. True, the number of women in full-time courses rose from 37,000 to 43,000. But as she pointed out, many women have commitments that make it impossible to go full-time. A lot of women could, however, benefit from a part-time course. While the Nationalists congratulate themselves on free higher education for all, they somehow neglect to mention this huge cutback in further education. They promise free childcare for one year olds upwards in an independent Scotland, but cut back on the opportunities for women to educate themselves for a better job when they are free to seek work. And, of course, no mention of the many jobs lost in Further Education. Labour is accused of casting aside the principle of universality. The Nationalists clearly do not believe in it themselves. If so, why would they grossly reduce opportunities for women who are simply hoping for decently paid work, while funding free university education for school leavers whose parents are wealthy enough to have sent them to fee-paying schools? You either fund all of it, because provision must be universal, or you don't, because at present the funds to do it are not there. In which case you make choices. You decide priorities.

As for childcare, what a dog's breakfast. First the Nationalists claim it will be funded, at a cost of £7000,000 per year, from the income tax paid by 100,000 women newly into work, plus that of the 35,000 newly employed in childcare. When it is shown by the Scottish Parliament's own information service that the true cost is some £1.2 billion, before building and equipment are included, they then pluck further savings from getting rid of Trident. But their own White Paper makes it clear that Trident will not go any time soon, and certainly not in good time to fund the promised levels of childcare. The SNP has been promising better pre-school childcare for over seven years, and now, due to Barnett 'consequentials' (meaning money from the Treasury), they will at last make a start. Otherwise, they tell us, we have to wait for independence for full delivery for one year olds upwards, because if done under devolution, all the income taxes gained from women getting into paid jobs would be handed over to the UK Treasury. A strange argument. When Salmond makes efforts to win more jobs for Scotland, does he curtail his efforts on the grounds that these new employees (later estimated at only 60,000 by the Scottish Parliament researchers) would have their income taxes paid into, and I quote, 'George Osborne's back pocket'? Of course not. People would think he was mad. So why are these women's jobs being treated differently? What was really striking, though, was the belief that this would be enough to win over women voters. Unfortunately, women were not particularly impressed by the idea of going out to work while some other woman was paid to look after her children, and then find there's not much help available when they start school.

Some years ago, the STUC Women's Committee created a parody of The Proclaimers' song:

When Ah hoover, Ah know Ah'm gonny be
the one who also cooks and scrubs the flair.
When Ah'm cleaning, Ah know that Ah can dream
of a society that's really fair.

YES, in Natland it is dreams. Nicola Sturgeon goes around the country painting rosy pictures of all our dreams coming true, while Alex Salmond designs an economic policy that owes more to George Osborne than it does to Keynes.

Given that past performance is a fairly reliable guide to future conduct, the Nationalist record comes nowhere near that of Labour's in getting things done for women.

It was the Labour Party that created the Equal Pay Act, and Harriet

Harman has spelled out ways to deliver it when the next Labour Government is elected, such as requiring employers to publish their pay structure, thereby making it easier for unequally paid staff to pursue their case. It was Labour that brought in the National Minimum Wage, and promotes the Living Wage now throughout the economy, not just in the public sector. The White Paper says the National Minimum Wage is to be protected, and the Living Wage promoted, but there is no mention of equal pay. That has not stopped Nicola Sturgeon from promising action when she addressed the Engender Conference in March. Nothing specific, though. So why is it not in the White Paper? Because they are saying one thing to business and another to underpaid women. However, not to worry if you are a director or outright owner of a large business. Your cut in corporation tax, for which grateful thanks to Alex Salmond for bringing it below where even George Osborne would set it, will vastly improve your income. Too bad if poorly paid women and men take an unfair share of the burden you have been relieved of.

At the time when the Scottish Parliament was being created, there was considerable controversy over issues like abortion and embryo research. Some wanted abortion law to be devolved, in anticipation that tighter controls would be enforced in line with Scotland's more conservative attitudes. So much for the notion that Scotland is more progressive than England. The plain fact is that in Westminster, with free votes and no whipping by any political party, there have been large majorities against tightening the current abortion law, and for obtaining the benefits of embryo research. At one stage Scottish clan chiefs, holding hereditary membership of the House of Lords, tried to persuade the House of Commons that a child born of artificial insemination by a donor should not inherit the title of clan chieftain and inherit a place in the House of Lords. As Peter Thurnham, a Conservative MP who sat on the committee with me, pointed out to the Lairds' great discomfiture, the science of DNA has shown that the real father of quite a number of children is not the man named on the birth certificate. Therefore, by their own logic, there are already a number of Lords who ought not to be hereditary peers. When I hear an English Tory MP being more progressive than a Scottish clan chief, I really do wonder why anyone thinks Scotland is ahead of England in social attitudes. Considering Alex Salmond, when he was an

MP as well as an MSP, took a trip to Westminster to vote to curtail abortion rights, it would be interesting if some pollster would find out, before we vote on 18 September, where current SNP MSPs and MPs stand on such issues. There is nothing to be learned in the White Paper. Merely the words: 'There are no plans to change the current abortion time limit.' Those who remember *Yes, Minister* with affection will remember that this is politician speak for giving hope to one side while giving false assurance to the other. It is noticeable that the ultra-lefts in the YES campaign have been strangely quiet on such issues.

The White Paper repeatedly claims that an independent Scotland will be a fairer Scotland. It also claims Westminster is no use and never has been. This is an absurd and ignorant claim. Let us just run through a brief list, off the top of my head.

- Votes for women, and working-class men. In 2014 it is timely to remember that men who had no vote and no say had their lives sacrificed in the First World War.

- The Married Women's Property Act, ending centuries of women being exploited financially by their husbands.

- Equal rights for women to education up to the highest levels.

- Barring married women from jobs such as teaching made unlawful.

- Family Allowances (later termed child benefit) paid to the mother, widows' pensions, single parent benefits, tax credits.

- The NHS and the Welfare State.

- The Equal Pay and Sex Discrimination Acts. No more sacking a woman on grounds of pregnancy.

- The National Minimum Wage.

- The 1967 Abortion Law reform, saving women from do-it-your-self and back street abortionists.

- The creation of the Scottish Parliament, opening up opportunities for women to have equal representation. Only Labour, however, has delivered equal numbers of men and women.

If any leading Scottish Nationalist took any part in any of the above, maybe they would like to tell us about it. As it is, I read Winnie Ewing's memoirs recently, and saw no mention by her of any participation in improving the lot of women.

So, how would the SNP build on these achievements? The White Paper mentions the need for more women on public boards, but has nothing to say on the dearth of women in the ranks of their MSPs. No wonder. When the Scottish Parliament was created 15 years ago, the Nationalists played no part in the battle for women's representation at a level comparable to the Scandinavian countries. (Interesting that they constantly hold up these countries as examples of what we could achieve, but never in that respect.) In subsequent elections the share enjoyed by their women has actually fallen substantially.

To sum up: I see in the UK a long history of achievement to the benefit of the many, through struggle by trade unions (who, let us not forget, had to battle to win legal existence), political parties, individual MPs who promoted worthy causes, petitions and single-issue campaigns. Nothing was handed down from on high. If this Tory-led Government were to win the next election, there would be even more rolling back of such achievements. Fortunately, they can be thrown out of office very soon, by a public fed up with millionaires getting tax cuts while the working population have their wages held down. Fed up with hospital waiting lists getting longer again. Fed up with house prices rising beyond belief. Fed up with ever-rising energy bills. The SNP hope the Tories will look like being on course to win the next General Election because that serves their cause. Never mind if people endure the miseries of food banks, rising heating bills, wage cuts and much else besides meanwhile. However, people should remember that the Tories last won a General Election outright as long ago as 1992. There will be voters in this referendum who were not even born then. Nor is it true that the whole of England is more Conservative-minded than Scotland. If you believe that, try a trip to Liverpool or Durham, or the working-class areas of London.

Creating a new state in itself does nothing to resolve our problems of child poverty, unemployment and unfair distribution of wealth. These matters are not dealt with merely by putting a cross in the box marked YES. Life is a bit harder than that. We need to face up to such realities, and not daydream about jam tomorrow, delivered by a single vote in a referendum. If we want to help our fellow citizens to a better life, then we need to stand up, not stand aside.

MARIA FYFE was formerly the Labour MP for Glasgow Maryhill (1987–2001). Before that, she was a Glasgow District Councillor. Previously, she was a Further Education lecturer in trade union studies. She is widowed, and has two sons and four grandchildren. She was a founder member of the Scottish Constitutional Convention and the convenor of its Working Group on Women's Issues. She is a campaigner for equal representation in councils and parliaments. She is the author of *A Problem Like Maria*, a reminiscence of her days in male-dominated Westminster.

CHAPTER 6

A Historic Union to Keep and Cherish

TRISH GODMAN

I AM DEEPLY opposed to the Nationalist campaign to separate Scotland from England, Wales and Northern Ireland.

After years of activity as a trade union and Labour Party member, shop steward, Councillor and latterly MSP, I am convinced that we on the left must campaign for a NO vote. The people of Scotland are in a strong partnership with the citizens of the other nations of the UK. We benefit enormously from our two parliaments. We simply cannot afford to gamble with the separation of Scotland from this family of nations. We do not have to choose between being Scottish and being British. We can be both in a modern Scotland and Britain.

Let me say that I do not condemn those who argue for separation. One of my closest friends is a passionate advocate for a separate Scotland, but our discussions – arguments even – are conducted in a civilised manner that would have earned the approval of the late Margo Macdonald.

Those Nationalists who argue their case *ad hominem* will dismiss someone like me as an unthinking lackey of the Tory Party's 'Union' campaign. On the other hand, that tiny handful of Marxist nationalists may regard me more sympathetically as one of many Labour activists suffering from false consciousness. I say – let them get on with it.

I take great pride in being a Glaswegian, as well as being Scottish and British. I'm also intensely proud of the many political, economic and social reforms achieved by Scottish, Welsh and English members of our labour movement down the years.

I do not forget that in the face of intense hostility from the Tory Party, a Labour Government led by an English Prime Minister and wholeheartedly supported by British ministers and back-benchers created the National Health Service.

I have a continuing pride in and respect for the NHS. All of my life, I have had a close connection to the health service. When I was three, my mother was diagnosed with TB. In those days there was no cure. When I look back now I know my father would not have been able to look after my brother and myself, and work, had it not been for the local 'green lady' and the nurse who attended to my mother three or four days a week.

Years later, when working with those people who had mental health problems, I witnessed again the dedication, care and commitment from those employed in the NHS. We have the best of all worlds with our NHS administered as it is from Edinburgh by way of our devolved parliament.

When Nationalists complain of the lack of social justice displayed by an uninterested Westminster elite, they ignore the socially liberalising and radical acts introduced by the Labour Government in the 1960s. David Steel would never have succeeded with his Private Member's Bill on a woman's right to have an abortion without the support and co-operation of the Home Secretary Roy Jenkins and other Labour members. Similarly, that administration liberalised divorce legislation and abolished the cruel, legal persecution of homosexuals.

As a social worker in the East End of Glasgow, my work with people in need benefitted dramatically by the implementation of the Social Work (Scotland) Act 1968. This was a remarkable and novel piece of legislation that improved our social work services and helped improve numerous lives. For example, it gave us the Children's Hearing system. It put us ahead of most other advanced nations in the way we dealt with children and young people. Radical legislation for Scotland enacted in Westminster.

This legislation was the work of the late Willie Ross, supported by his British parliamentary colleagues. Willie Ross was known throughout Britain as a leading member of the Wilson administration and more than capable of defending and promoting the interests of the Scottish people, especially those in need. The Bill was navigated through its committee stages by the Edinburgh MP, Ted Willis, born and raised in Norwich but who came to Scotland from the south of England.

During the miners' dispute in the 1980s, this Act of Parliament was courageously employed by the then Strathclyde Regional Council's Director of Social Work, the late Professor Fred Edwards, another migrant from England. Or perhaps, as Alasdair Gray would have it, an 'English settler.'

'Fred Ed,' as he was known, was able to use sections of this Act in order to provide assistance to the children of miners' families suffering deep financial distress.

I readily acknowledge that both Labour and Tory governments have made grievous errors of judgement that have harmed the lives of Scots, English, Welsh and Northern Ireland citizens. I need hardly remind you of Mrs Thatcher's destruction of the coal mining industry, and the calamitous Poll Tax. The latter obliterated largely by popular protest in both Scotland and in England.

We also had the disastrous decision of Mr Blair to participate in the invasion of Afghanistan and Iraq. Despite these horrible errors of judgement, I believe that today we have a stronger Westminster Parliament much more willing to tackle the Executive and, at the same time, a Scottish Parliament that protects and promotes the interests of all Scots in wide ranging areas of public and community life.

A more recent Labour Government in Westminster introduced the National Minimum Wage, kept us out of the Euro and introduced other measures that have made life much more tolerable for the vast majority of the British people. Nationalists will say that all of that is now history: 'Time to move on.'

Which is precisely what Labour did with the creation of the Scottish Parliament.

Whatever you may think of the Parliament's architectural design, I believe that, as a devolved legislature, it has been a success. One that should be followed elsewhere. I say that on the basis of my experience as an MSP. I had the privilege and the satisfaction, as the convener of the local government committee, in assisting with the abolition of the detested 'Section 28,' which sought to discriminate against employment of homosexuals in the public sector, and the banning of the dreaded poindings and warrant sales.

Similarly, legislation such as Adults with Incapacity Act 2000, Mental Care and Treatment Act 2003 and the Smoking ban were all streets ahead of other legislatures and passed by successive administrations. This is how it should be with a devolved Parliament with extensive authority over legal, educational, health and other areas that have a significant influence on the everyday life of Scots. We have a unique Scottish Parliament that is growing in stature.

In this family of four nations, much can be learned and adopted by our English friends and relatives in relation to the developments in Edinburgh, Cardiff and Stormont. I need hardly say that the relationships among these four have been fractious in recent times, but both my head and my heart tell me that we are better together than living in separate nations.

If we in Scotland have worries over distant political elites laying down the law to us, it is not Westminster to which we should direct our attention, but to the undemocratic European Union. The principle of subsidiarity (the devolution of political decision making to national parliaments and local authorities) is conspicuously ignored by those in Brussels. Radical change is needed anent the European Court of Justice, the Common Agricultural Policy, the Common Fisheries Policy, subsidiarity and the nonsensical idea of an EU defence and foreign office.

This radical reform will not be achieved by small nations. We need a strong and cohesive British Parliament to challenge the EU administration and the political elite. We need our four-member Britain to campaign vigorously for substantial change in the EU. We must seek radical change from a position of strength and influence.

Turning to other matters, I am deeply sceptical over the unthoughtful assertions made by the separatists that, with separation, all will be well with the sharing of the pound, the protection – perhaps the enhancement – of pensions and welfare, and maintenance, or even expansion of our industries. What of defence, defence industries and immigration? Would we, with separation, be an EU member state immediately? Or, for several years, be an applicant for membership? At the same time it is somewhat odd to campaign for separation whilst adhering to British monetary policy. What would happen to the pound? There are no substantive statements on these important issues, only assertions with no reinforcing evidence.

I agree with Lord Reid of Cardowan when he says: 'If you want a divorce then don't pretend you can keep the benefits of marriage.'

Admittedly, it's difficult to be enthusiastic and passionate when saying No. Nevertheless, you can be committed to, and feel both affection and respect for our four-member nation with its history, its cultures, its values, its toleration of minority interests and groups, its civilities and its shared stoicism and courage in times of adversity. We can, however, remain uniquely Scottish in this nation of four.

As a Glaswegian, I have a deep affection for my city, for Scotland and other members of this nation of Britain. I want to remain a member of this historic union of people, so I will vote NO on the day.

TRISH GODMAN was born in Govan, left school at 15, took on various jobs, and was a single mother of three sons. In 1980, she married Norman Godman, who a few years later became a highly regarded MP, now retired. Aged 37, she went to Jordanhill College and qualified as a social worker and worked in the East End of Glasgow. She became a NALGO shop steward, then Strathclyde Regional Councillor, and later Glasgow City Councillor. In 1999 she became MSP, then Deputy Presiding Officer of the Scottish Parliament. Since leaving the Parliament, she has been active in voluntary associations and any spare time is given over to her allotment.

CHAPTER 7

An Internationalist View

KAINDE MANJI

FOR ME, THE decision to vote NO in the forthcoming referendum was not an obvious or straightforward one. I have lived in Scotland for ten years and feel very much that Scotland is my home. Many of the significant events of my life have taken place here. I studied here as an undergraduate, I have worked here, and am now studying here again for my PhD. I met my husband here when we were both undergraduates, and ten years later it was the natural choice that we would get married in our hometown of Stirling, the place we have built our lives together. At the end of last year we also made the momentous and for us (and many of our generation) very unexpected step of buying property here. But anyone who was to hear me speak would judge immediately that I am not Scottish. I speak with a somewhat plummy southern counties accent that has been the bane of my existence since my school days.

Neither, despite the accent, do I really identify as English. I lived in Oxford between the ages of nine and 20, and completed most of my schooling there, but for me Englishness has always had rather uncomfortable connotations of skinheads and football hooligans, or the twee image of Morris dancers on the village green. Britishness too, has never been an identity I felt particularly easy to adopt. I was born in Kenya, as were my parents, and as were three of my grandparents. Before that my family came from India. We are products of a colonial history where Britishness had come to represent control and oppression. At the same time, it was these historic ties that allowed my grandfather, the eldest of 12 children (of whom only nine survived to adulthood) from a not particularly wealthy Nairobi family, to travel to the UK to train to be a pharmacist. There he met my grandmother, a young woman from Rhyl in North Wales, who was allowed to attend University only because the University of London had been evacuated to Cardiff during the war. However, when the war ended it was to Kenya they returned, establishing the country's first 'multi-racial' school in their garden; and at Independence from colonial rule in 1963 they were both committed to working to build the new Kenya.

Britishness then is for me a conflicted identity. While I am proud of my African heritage, I have lived in the UK for long enough now that I can make little claim to be culturally Kenyan. However, though I feel strongly that Scotland is my home, and the place I hope to spend the rest of my life, I have not yet lived here long enough to be widely recognised and accepted by many as Scottish. I suppose British is the best description of what I am. But rather like the claymore wielding, plaid wearing, vehemently nationalist Scot, conceptions of Englishness and Britishness that I painted before are really little more than stereotype. The people involved in YES (for the most part) bear as little relation to the see-you-jimmy stereotype as I do to the jolly-hockey-sticks, Home Counties stereotype that my accent suggests. Though identity inevitably plays a part, this referendum is about much, much more than that.

On a personal level, I prefer to think of myself as an internationalist, eschewing the ties of national identity. As a result, the European focus and internationalist rhetoric of the YES campaign could appear attractive. However, I cannot help but feel that these positions are fundamentally at odds with the decision we are being faced with. The cause of nationalism in itself is an inherently inward-looking perspective.

Nor do I buy the argument that the only way for Scotland to rid itself of Tory oppression is to become independent and establish a new welfare state on social democratic principles in the model of the Nordic nations. My reaction to this is both emotional and intellectual. As a product of colonialism, I cannot help but feel offended at the associations implied between the acts of austerity by the present UK Government – which are without doubt causing unnecessary misery for thousands of people across the country – and the acts of British colonial governments which in Kenya alone involved forced imprisonment, torture, and other atrocities the extent of which is only now, 70 years on, coming to light (Cobain & Norton-Taylor, 2012). I don't feel these allusions do justice to either case. The legality of some of the cuts has rightly been called into question, and there are indeed strong grounds to protest under both international and European Human Rights law, but the democratic and legal process in this country is enabling these cases to be heard. The debate is open and free, and in 2015 we will have the opportunity to overturn the government peacefully at the polls. The same could not be said for Kenya in the 1950s, and it is unhelpful to conflate the two. It should also not be forgotten that Scottish people played an active part within British colonial administrations the world over. Independence from the UK will not conveniently absolve us of these past sins.

I take issue with the argument from a more intellectual perspective too. Since joining the campaign for a NO vote, I have been asked to speak on various platforms and in various fora. Time and again I have heard the argument that the present constitutional arrangements, because Scotland returned only one Conservative MP at the 2010 General Election, are deeply undemocratic. The existence of the solitary Tory is indisputable, but the present Government is a coalition involving the Liberal Democrats, including Chief Secretary to the Treasury and Scottish MP Danny Alexander. Elected in Scotland with Scottish votes.

The argument that independence would rid us of the scourge of Toryism once and for all is also rather problematic, when one considers the Scottish Parliament. In 1997 not a single Scottish constituency returned a Conservative MP at the General Election. As my husband likes to say, 'Scotland was a Tory-free zone.' However, by 1999, with the creation of the Scottish Parliament and a new, more proportionate electoral system, there were 18 Scottish Conservative MSPs. This decreased slightly to 17 in 2007, and then 15 in 2011, but overall the Conservatives have remained a remarkably stable presence in the Scottish Parliament since devolution. They may never obtain enough votes to form a government, but they certainly proved useful to the SNP minority administration in key votes after 2007, and it is not inconceivable that they could form part of a future coalition.

The argument that Scottish people are inherently more social democratic than the rest of the UK does not hold strong either. Research by Keating (2005) suggests that while the Scottish Parliament has adopted some divergent policy approaches, such as Free Personal Care for the elderly and the abolition of university tuition fees, this is not matched by a stronger predisposition for social democratic policies in public opinion. More recently, research by Curtice and Ormston (2011) using the Scottish and British Social Attitudes Surveys found only modestly more support for social democratic measures in Scotland. Interestingly, they also found that the Scottish Parliament has become less rather than more social democratic in its approach to policy over time.

The social democratic 'utopia' of the Nordic countries has also come under threat in recent times. Both Sweden and Norway have seen Social Democrats struggle at the polls, and cuts to spending on the welfare state have been witnessed across the region, as they have here. The forces of globalisation and an international financial crisis have left their mark on even those countries with the strongest traditions of social democratic welfarism. The path to a social democratic independent Scotland would therefore be a rocky one, set against the backdrop of the external pressures of an increasingly interdependent global market.

Even were this likely to be a smooth transition, I suppose I would ask: why Scotland alone? I am not persuaded by the argument that austerity has been somehow more severe in Scotland than it has been in England. We are all facing the realities of austerity. It cannot be denied that the impact of the cuts and so-called 'reforms' to the benefits system will be staggering. Though many of the proposed changes are yet to take hold, many others, such as the Bedroom Tax, have been implemented, and the effects are already being felt. Similarly, while the Government's flagship Universal Credit has been beset by technical problems relating to the complex IT system it will be supported by, some of the more punitive sanctions regimes associated with it have already been put in place. But is this really worse in Scotland? Recent research into levels of 'workless-ness' and associated social problems compared Glasgow and Middles-brough, and found strong similarities in the patters of cyclical unem-ployment and churning arising from long-term unemployment and de-industrialisation (Schildrick et al, 2012). If the context that the reforms are being implemented in is the same, the impact is likely to be too. Similarly, research by Beatty and Fothergill (2013) found that high numbers of incapacity benefit claimants (one of the main targets of reform) were concentrated in areas that had experienced de-industrial-isation across the UK. What then of the residents of Liverpool, Manches-ter, Middlesbrough, Gateshead, Sunderland and Carlisle?

It seems to me that what is needed is a change of government, not a change of country. The challenges we face are multiple and grave. They should not be underestimated. They have also been made particularly cruel by the implementation of savage cuts to public spending by a party bent on capitalising on the age of austerity for ideological reasons (Farnsworth & Irving, 2012). But these challenges are by no means unique to Scotland, or even to the UK. Similar scenes have been witnessed in Spain, Italy, Greece and Ireland. When I have made this case in the context of debates with supporters of the YES campaign, I have been told that my argument is spurious. That an independent Scotland will still express solidarity with those in England, as we do with countries in crisis in Southern Europe. In fact, they argue that the English will be as liberated by our departure as we will. But is solidarity with Spain really the same? Will passive solidarity really be enough for those denied the opportunity to work with people in Scotland for a collective solution? One that benefits not just those of us north of Hadrian's Wall, but the whole of the UK.

So while I find the arguments by supporters of a YES vote that independence would give us an opportunity to develop novel solutions to some of these global problems attractive, I can't help feeling that those arguments are somewhat limited, and rather exclusive if they apply to only a lucky few north of the border. Maybe it is time to be really radical. Maybe it is time not to seek out a new national identity in the form of a new nation, but to create a new unifying identity for the whole United Kingdom. A new form of Britishness. One I think I could happily identify with.

KAINDE MANJI is a feminist and disability rights activist who has worked across the equalities sector in Scotland. She has campaigned on a range of issues affecting women including childcare funding for student parents, the representation of women in Scottish politics, and against the gender pay gap. She is currently working for a PhD at the University of Glasgow.

References

Beatty, C. and Fothergill, S., 'Disability benefits in the UK: an issue of jobs or health?' in Lindsay, C. and Houston, D. eds. *Disability Benefits, Welfare Reform and Employment Policy*. (Hampshire: Palgrave Macmillan, 2013).

Curtice, J. and Ormston, R., 'Is Scotland more left-wing than England?' *British Social Attitudes 28* (Special Edition No.42. Glasgow: ScotCen, 2011).

Cobain, I. and Norton-Taylor, R., 'Sins of colonialists lay concealed for decades in secret archive' *The Guardian*, Wednesday 18 April. Available at: http://www.theguardian.com/uk/2012/apr/18/sins-colonialists-concealed- secret-archive [accessed on 17.01.14]

Farnsworth, K. and Irving, Z., 'Varieties of crisis, varieties of austerity: Social Policy in challenging times'. *Journal of Poverty and Social Justice 20* (2, 2012). pp. 133–147

Keating, M., 'Policy Convergence and divergence in Scotland under devolution' *Regional Studies* 39 (4, 2005)). pp. 453–463.

Schildrick, T., MacDonald, R., Furlong, A., Roden, J., and Crow, R., eds. *Are 'Cultures of Worklessness' passed down the generations?* (York: Joseph Rowntree, 2012)

CHAPTER 8

A Gamble with our Livelihood and Welfare

RONNIE MCDONALD

I WANT A positive future for my country, with a strong, healthy economy, where life choices for our children are optimistic and secure, where equality, justice, fairness and democracy are the principles which bind us together.

2014 is the year when voters living in Scotland will either vote for independence or stay with devolution. We will decide whether to be an independent country or remain as a country within the UK, as we have for more than 300 years.

Around 800,000 first generation Scots who have chosen to live and work in other parts of the UK will be excluded from voting in the referendum. Many identify themselves, first and foremost, as being Scottish. Just ask Billy Connolly or Alex Ferguson what nationality they are. Their national identity isn't questioned for a moment. Even Rod Stewart has adopted Scotland and its national football team, and all because his dad was Scottish. And, in turn, Scotland has adopted Rod Stewart.

Yet the invidious position of the SNP is that unless you support separation you are somehow anti-Scottish, are against Scotland. Being proud of being Scottish does not involve territorial boundaries.

Back in the day, I was one of many who campaigned for a Scottish Parliament and had the privilege of co-ordinating the 50/50 campaign, to try to secure equal representation of women and men in our new Parliament.

It was the STUC Women's Committee who first proposed 50/50 gender equality. It was a truly bold proposal for its time, but our view was that if Scotland was to have its own Parliament, then women should take their equal place alongside men in shaping the future of our country.

However, forever the pragmatists, we knew that if we were to have any hope of achieving this, we would need the support of the trade union and labour movement. So a handful of women trade unionists and Labour Party women came together informally, and worked within their respective organisations to secure their democratic support for equal representation.

That mandate was essential to the campaign and six months after it was first proposed, 50/50 gender balance was adopted as policy by the STUC Annual Congress and the Scottish Labour Party Conference.

The women's committee initiated a number of different strands to win public support for 50/50 and equality in the devolution debate. We established the Women's Co-ordination Group, bringing together like-minded women to engage with civic society. We initiated a series of informal and formal discussions with women and men from the main political parties.

Within the WCG, we had an appealing campaign to reach out to women and men through local events. We prepared briefing and campaign materials and posters, organised public and media events, struck a series of 50/50 badges and even had a 50/50 song.

There was a groundswell of public opinion in favour of devolution. The SNP didn't want devolution and played little part in the campaign to secure increased powers for the people of Scotland. The Conservatives wanted nothing to do with it and played no part at all.

But the people of Scotland, different and diverse in so many ways, came together to support the call for devolution. A range of conferences on key issues, which we knew could be improved upon if we secured devolved powers, were organised. We placed adverts in the national press, funded by women and men whose common link was for a new democracy based on equality and fairness.

Research and discussion with other regional states helped inform our debate. We met European leaders, national presidents and government leaders and presented our case for devolution. We were united in our support for better, not separate governance for Scotland.

We came together as trade union, political party, local government, churches, academic, women and voluntary organisation representatives in the Scottish Constitutional Convention to work together to establish the basic principles for a new democracy for our country.

Our discussions with politicians were crucial for the campaign for 50/50. Within the SCC, the Labour Party and the Scottish Liberal Democrats signed up to an electoral pact in which they agreed to select and field equal numbers of men and women candidates for election to a Scottish Parliament.

On 1 May 1997 the Labour Government was elected and one of the first major pieces of legislation put through Parliament by that Labour Government was the Scotland Act 1998 which delivered devolution for Scotland.

However, at the first Scottish Parliament election, only the Labour Party operated a specific mechanism to achieve gender balance in representation. The SNP rejected specific measures to increase women's representation.

The devolved powers were significant. Right from the outset there were tax-varying powers of up to three pence. Major issues affecting crucial aspects of our lives are decided upon in Scotland in education and training, environment, health and social services, housing, law and legal matters, local government, sport, tourism and many more.

Our Parliament has achieved so much. The lives of many people have been enriched as a consequence of the devolution settlement and many radical and farsighted policies have been introduced since its inception – from the early introduction of free care for the elderly to the recent Equal Marriage Act.

As a woman trade union official, I worked to improve the economic, social and political rights of women. But women remain discriminated against. And, yes, we know there is much still to be done to create a fair and equal society.

So I ask myself what are the big issues facing us today? What, if anything, can we predict for the future? For me action on equality, social justice, poverty and democracy remain essential.

Increased globalisation and the digital revolution have changed our world. Climate change and sustainability are crucial issues for all of us. Our global population today is over seven billion. Personal wealth is distributed so unevenly across the world, with the richest two per cent owning more than 50 per cent of the world's assets. More than a third of the world lives in poverty. For everyone, sudden and unexpected poverty has become a real possibility in the developed world.

The SNP wants Scotland to be independent. It wants fiscal autonomy but wants to keep the pound sterling as our currency, to be policed by the Bank of England. The SNP wants equality for Scotland, but wants to retain that bastion of inequality, the hereditary monarchy as our head of state. It wants to continue to be a member of the European Union but can't guarantee that we won't need to join the queue with other European countries wanting to be members. Its White Paper offers guarantees on the continued broadcasting of television soaps, but is a lot less convincing on economic issues.

The White Paper has been called a work of fiction and there are serious doubts that the SNP has got the sums right for the funding of an independent Scotland. It is clear that Scotland would have a huge immediate debt, that oil revenue would be wholly insufficient to pay for that debt, and that an independent Scottish government would face higher interest charges on new loans than the UK.

It looks to me that the SNP want independence-lite, that the SNP is feart.

I believe that rather than increase our democracy and democratic rights, an SNP independent Scotland would become less democratic. I have the right to vote in local government, Scottish, Westminster, and European elections. I have the right to vote for the political parties whom I believe are best suited to deliver my vision of a better society.

If Scotland becomes independent-lite, I'm not allowed to vote in the Westminster elections and probably not eligible to vote in the European elections either. Two powerful democratic forums, which make immensely crucial decisions affecting our lives, would both be out of our reach.

And there is no overture in the proposals of the SNP that heralds an improved democracy for women, where measures would be available to increase women's representation in an independent Scottish Parliament.

The primary role of any government is to provide stability for its people, to provide institutional stability to enable all sectors to work effectively. Any political party which seeks to implement a policy which will, either as its primary purpose or as a side effect of achieving its primary purpose, create institutional instability, must demonstrate to an exacting standard of proof that it has thoughtfully considered and sought to mitigate the impact of this instability.

The SNP cannot confirm with certainty which currency we will use, nor which supranational organisations we will be members of. As such, regardless of whether you like the idea of independence in the abstract or not, it is clear that despite having had many years to prepare, the SNP have roundly failed to provide more than the most superficial case for independence. They are prepared to gamble with our livelihood and welfare.

Increased powers have already been secured for the Scottish Parliament since it was first created. It has been further empowered from 2015 with additional tax raising and borrowing powers. Our country doesn't need to cede the strength and security of the UK to evolve. We are currently able to channel political decisions to meet local needs and this would continue with the status quo. Our democratic processes will constantly change to meet the ever increasing challenges we face.

I do not support the present Coalition Government, and abhor the divisive policies it is implementing, as do many of my friends and neighbours here and in other parts of the UK. But we can currently vote to change governing parties as well as continue to have representation in that political process.

I do not support shallow, narrow-minded, ill-informed nationalist views that my country must be independent to prosper. I believe it does a huge disservice to the people of Scotland for the SNP to simply throw a tantrum on the big economic issues of currency union, debt, membership of the European Union and the affordability of breaking up the United Kingdom. They are displaying the logic of a young child when faced with something they don't want to hear, in the hope that it will all turn out right in the end.

The franchise – votes for working people, for women – was hard fought. We deserve more honesty from those seeking to change the destiny of Scotland. The achievement of 37 per cent women's representation in the first Scottish Parliament was a journey by many, a narrative of endeavour and challenge alike. It was a key part of enhancing our democracy.

Come 18 September, we have the opportunity to influence how our country develops. I do not want to risk the uncertainty of my family having to suffer for the next 50 years or more for the ideology of a political party that wants separation despite the many imponderables the SNP can't answer, let alone resolve.

In our highly networked world, we know our immediate neighbours face similar challenges to those we face, but we also know that for many across the globe there are challenges of war and poverty and want.

The big issues facing our planet need to be addressed. And bigger and powerful alliances can help to influence big decisions. Scotland, my country on its own, will have little influence on big issues. I want my grandson to be proud to be Scottish and to be an international player. I want him to have a future, and YES, I'll be voting NO.

RONNIE MCDONALD was Deputy General Secretary at the STUC having previously been Assistant Secretary, developing campaigns and policies for improving equality and fairness for women in the social, political and economic life of Scotland. She worked with, and was a member of, various equality bodies, including the Scottish Committee of the Equality and Human Rights Commission. Ronnie established the Women's Co-ordination Group to campaign for equal representation in the first Scottish Parliament elections. She received the CBE for services to equal opportunities in Scotland, which she accepted on behalf of all the other campaigning women she worked with. Since retiring, Ronnie is a lifelong learner, an Italian student, a cyclist, artist and tennis player. And, most importantly, she tries to answer the many and varied questions her five-year-old grandson poses every other day!

CHAPTER 9

Scottish or British or Both?

JEAN MCFADDEN

THE IMPENDING REFERENDUM forces me to reflect on who I am. What is my identity? Have I had a constant identity or has it changed over the years? Am I Scottish or British or both? Or am I something more? Does identity have to be equated with nationality?

It was not something I ever thought of when I was a child. If I had been asked if I was Scottish or British I would not have known what to say (just as I didn't know what to say when I was taken aside by some big girls when I was about five and asked whether I was a Protestant or a Catholic). My school education was excellent and I was taught Scottish, English and British history, language and literature. If pushed, I would have said I was Scottish and British – but I was never asked and I never asked myself.

As a young student at Glasgow University in the 1960s, I regularly attended the debates in the Men's(!) Union, where the big hitters were Donald Dewar and John Smith for Labour, Neil MacCormick for the SNP, Ming Campbell for the Liberals, and Len Turpie for the Tories. This opened my eyes to British and Scottish politics and I became aware of Scottish nationalism – but I was not drawn to the SNP. They seemed to concentrate on ancient wrongs like the Clearances and the Stone of Destiny's removal to London, 700 years ago. Neil MacCormick's father, John, had been involved in the audacious attempt to bring it back to Scotland in 1950. He also brought the famous case of MacCormick v the Lord Advocate, which challenged the Queen's title of Queen Elizabeth II instead of Queen Elizabeth I of Scotland. Most folk are not aware of this, but postboxes in Scotland do not have ER II on them and the Queen signs herself simply Elizabeth R on official Scottish documents. Interesting issues and escapades at the time – but I didn't in any way feel oppressed by the English. I was becoming much more aware of class differences north and south of the border, rather than differences of nationality. I knew that I had more in common with the ordinary people of England than I did with the lairds and landowners of Scotland.

However, students at Glasgow University in the 1960s had a more international outlook and this rubbed off on me. In 1962, we elected Chief Albert Luthuli as Rector of Glasgow University. Chief Luthuli was President of the African National Congress and an early fighter for the anti-apartheid movement. That experience as a student influenced me almost 20 years later when, as Leader of Glasgow District Council, I succeeded in persuading the Council to confer the Freedom of the City of Glasgow on Nelson Mandela in 1981. This was received by the UK press with great hostility at the time, as Mandela was considered to be a terrorist, and the SNP kept their heads down, but I was proud that we had lifted our eyes beyond the confines of the city, and of the UK, to the oppressed people of South Africa. Another layer had been added to my identity.

And, of course, when the UK joined the Common Market in 1973, I also became a citizen of Europe.

So my identity is multi-layered, Scottish, British, European and international. But if Scotland votes for independence, I will lose my British citizenship, possibly my European citizenship (though not my international layer). But I like being British and European as well as Scottish and I don't want to give these up. In particular I share many values of the British and hundreds of years of history, including two World Wars. The recent commemoration of the D-Day landings in Normandy reinforced my dual identity as proud Scot and proud Briton. There are historical, social and cultural links that I do not want to see broken.

One of the consequences of Scottish independence will be the removal of all the MPs for Scottish constituencies from the Westminster Parliament. Only one of them is a Tory. A result could be to condemn the rest of the UK to Tory Governments for the foreseeable future. I would not want to inflict that on the ordinary people of England. Let's not forget that class issues still exist. At least the Welsh and the Northern Irish would be protected by their devolved Assemblies.

So I am going to vote NO to independence in the referendum this year, but not just because I want to keep my Britishness. The main reason? 'It's the economy, stupid,' as Bill Clinton's campaign manager said in 1991. I am not convinced by the financial arguments of the SNP that an independent Scotland would be better off than it is just now. But there is more to my view than the economic argument. I am not convinced that an independent Scotland would be a better place to live in than it is now, as part of the United Kingdom with a devolved Scottish Parliament in Edinburgh. I have been involved in Scottish politics and local government for nearly 50 years and that has taught me not to trust the SNP. They exhibit a disturbingly controlling and centralising attitude. For example, they have nationalised the Scottish Police and Fire Services and some aspects of education. Social Work services may also be in danger, too. They have more or less nationalised the council tax, a populist issue which gains them brownie points with the electorate but which undermines local government's already limited tax-raising powers and causes cuts in local services which hit the public hard and for which the councillors take the blame, not the Scottish Government. They pursue issues that benefit the rich more than the poor – free prescriptions for all, free university tuition for all. Yet they don't have the courage to use the tax-raising powers of the Scotland Act in case that might turn people off. But their current policies are financially unsustainable in the long term.

Locally, SNP councillors have little real interest in local government and seem to take their instructions from their masters in Edinburgh. They have no coherent local government policies and appear to see their sole role as ambassadors for nationalism instead of as the elected representatives of local people. In Glasgow, their behaviour at council meetings is deplorable. They show contempt for the Council and for the Lord Provost in the mistaken belief that she is a representative of the Queen.

As a Scot, I am annoyed that the SNP appear to claim a monopoly on patriotism and treat those of us who argue against them almost as traitors. I am as patriotic a Scot as they are, but I have a wider view of my homeland and my identity than they have.

I am annoyed that they have hi-jacked the Saltire. It's my flag too. And I am annoyed that they have tried to hi-jack Gaelic, the language of my late husband. To some extent, I feel oppressed by the SNP, not by the English.

And it was SNP MPs who voted with the Tories in 1979 to bring down the Labour Government and give us Mrs Thatcher, the Poll Tax and the decimation of Scottish industry. I have never forgiven them for that.

But Mrs T certainly did a wonderful job in increasing Scottishness and Scottish identity. I had voted against the proposed Scottish Assembly in 1979 because of the 'West Lothian Question,' but her policies and her treatment of Scotland made me a convert to devolution. The Campaign for a Scottish Assembly was formed by Labour Party Members with a few SNP supporters and led to the Scottish Constitutional Convention. As Vice President of the Convention of Scottish Local Authorities, I took part in the Scottish Constitutional Convention's inaugural meeting in 1989. The SNP attended but soon walked out and never came back. So much for having the good of the Scottish people at heart. Luckily that did not stop the SCC from producing a number of influential documents culminating in 1995 in 'Scotland's Parliament: Scotland's Right,' which acted as a basis for the Scotland Act 1998 and gave us the Scottish Parliament in 1999.

In my view devolution has been good for Scotland. The Scottish Parliament may have some flaws such as having adopted, to some extent, the 'yah-boo' politics of Westminster, but its existence has enabled Scottish legislation to be given the parliamentary time it deserves and could not get at Westminster because of its crowded timetable. As a result, great strides have been made in reforming many parts of Scots law, such as land law and mental health law – though there has been some poor drafting and a lack of the proper scrutiny which a second, revising chamber could address. But by and large the Scottish Parliament provides Scottish solutions for Scottish problems and the Calman Commission, set up by Labour, has resulted in increased powers for the Parliament and more control over taxation.

The existence of the Scottish Parliament has largely protected us from the policies of the Tory-Lib Dem coalition. If social security were added to the list of its powers, it could do even more to protect us. But I see no need to take over defence and the armed forces and we are better protected from terrorism by staying part of the UK.

However, the West Lothian Question has not gone away and the English are resentful that they alone in the UK have missed out on devolution. An English Parliament has always been ruled out so far, but the Westminster Government has to tackle this deficit, sooner rather than later.

The debate between YES and NO sides was somewhat sterile for the first months of this year. What has to be addressed urgently at some point this year is what constitutional changes should be proposed if independence is NOT supported by the majority of voters in Scotland. The Better Together campaign is a coalition of political parties whose policies do not normally coincide. We cannot expect Better Together to produce a unified proposal. But many undecided voters want answers. And now we have them from all the major political parties that support the Union. For all of them, the status quo is NOT an option.

The SNP deride these proposals from their opponents, telling voters that no party other than theirs can be trusted to deliver. Have they forgotten that the Labour Government, elected in 1997, delivered a referendum on a Scottish Parliament just months after the election, a Scotland Act in 1998 and the Scottish Parliament in 1999? Have they forgotten that Labour, with the support of the Tories and Lib-Dems, set up the Calman Commission in 2007 and the Tory/Lib-Dem coalition delivered more devolution in the Scotland Act 2012? I fear that all the SNP can deliver is the threat of never-ending referendums. A stronger Scottish Parliament or years of uncertainty? I know which option I prefer.

JEAN MCFADDEN was born and bred in Glasgow and has lived in Scotland all her life. She married John McFadden, who was brought up on the island of Barra and who was a fluent Gaelic speaker and broadcaster. She studied Classics at Glasgow University, gained a First Class Honours degree and became Principal Teacher of Classics in schools in Glasgow and Lanarkshire. With the decline of the Classics in schools, she was made redundant and took up the study of law at Strathclyde University. On graduating with a First Class Honours degree, she became a lecturer and later a senior lecturer in the Law School of Strathclyde University, specialising in constitutional and local government law. She is the author of books on Public Law, on the Scottish Parliament and on Scottish Local Government. She was elected to the Corporation of Glasgow in 1971, which became Glasgow District Council in 1975. She became Leader of the Labour Group in 1977 and Leader of the Council in 1979, the first woman to hold that post. She was Leader of the Council from 1979 to

1986, the period in which the regeneration of Glasgow as a post-industrial city began; City Treasurer from 1986 to 1992 and Leader again from 1992 to 1994. She has held the position of Depute Lord Lieutenant of the City of Glasgow since 1980. She was a founding member of the Scottish Constitutional Convention, which was formed in 1989. She was the first woman President of the Convention of Scottish Local Authorities (COSLA) from 1990 to 1992. She also chaired the Scottish Charity Law Review Commission, which resulted in the reform of Scots charity law with the enactment of the Charities and Trustee Investment (Scotland) Act 2005. Following the reorganisation of local government in 1995, she was elected to the newly constituted City of Glasgow Council. She was Chair of the Labour Group from 1995 to 2012. She held various high profile positions including the Convenorship of Strathclyde Joint Police Board and of the Social Strategy Committee. She was the Executive Member for Corporate Governance and later Executive Member for Education. She retired from the Council in 2012 but remains active in various areas of education, law and politics.

CHAPTER 10

So, what about the Pensioners?

ELINOR MCKENZIE

ACCORDING TO THE *Sunday Times* Rich List, the richest 1,000 people in Britain increased their collective assets in 2013/14 by 13 per cent, bringing their total wealth up to £518.9 billion. Interestingly, Scotland's 100 richest people on the list have 'surged to new heights,' with their wealth rising 19 per cent in the past year. The wealth of the top 104 exceeds the wealth of the other 896 people on the list put together. The *Sunday Times* list also shows that the collective wealth of the 1,000 most affluent people is a third of UK GDP (the value of all the goods and services we produce per year). Clearly, the billionaires are getting richer and the multibillionaires too.

So what does that mean for pensioners who are not insulated with inherited wealth, Big City speculation profits or gold plated pensions? It means that while the mega-rich get richer, many pensioners are struggling for survival in this so-called 'Age of Austerity.'

The number of UK pensioners living on pensions set below the poverty level exceeds 2.5 million, according to the Scottish Pensioners' Forum. Another group, the National Pensioners Convention has claimed that over ten pensioners die from cold related illnesses every hour during winter months in the UK. The biggest single factor in cold related illness is poverty.

Against this backdrop, on 18 September 2014, the Scottish electorate will vote on Scotland's constitutional future. There will be one question in this referendum – YES or NO to independence.

The debate is on, and the result of the referendum will have huge consequences for pensioners and indeed, the working class in Scotland and in other UK nations. From a left perspective, the test of any independence proposal is determined by which class interests are being served.

The Scottish Government, led by the Scottish National Party (SNP), recently produced a 650-page White Paper, 'Scotland's Future,' setting out the terms of independence. It proposes that a constitutionally independent Scotland will retain the monarchy, and join NATO. It will keep the pound within a currency union with the rest of Britain and it will remain part of the European Union (EU). Notwithstanding cautionary statements from Westminster and Brussels, this is the current position of the SNP. In essence, everything will remain the same, but everything will change.

We will have no MPs at Westminster to input on these UK-wide matters.

And how is the three-card trick to be worked? By letting us call it independence.

These proposals will form the basis for economic growth, a treaty of separation and for the constitution of an independent Scotland.

Does this matter? YES, the SNP's recipe for growth is to reduce tax on big business and 'high net-worth individuals.' This big business, neo-liberal perspective is also shared by the institutions that will in reality determine economic policy – the Bank of England and the European Union (EU) Commission.

The SNP is taking forward the traditional Tory view that by concentrating on economic growth, state intervention can be reduced on the assumption that creating a 'bigger cake' will benefit everyone. Clearly this 'trickle down' economic theory does not work. Identifying the root causes of poverty, and inequality, and finding real lasting solutions to such issues should be the number one priority for the Scottish Parliament.

While economic growth is certainly important to Scotland's future, it needs to be accompanied by increasing democratic control of the economy to make sure that the economic benefits are for the many and not the few entrepreneurs – Scottish or otherwise – who seem to be favoured by the SNP, whether in Scotland or elsewhere. Interestingly, significant public ownership just doesn't come into it!

Currently, the top 20 companies in Scotland – such as Standard Life, Scottish Widows, Scottish Southern Energy, to mention just three – are wholly owned subsidiaries of foreign multi-nationals and London Stock Exchange quoted corporations.

If we want to shift power from those who own the wealth to the workers and pensioners who created it, we need to act at the level where that power lies. Clearly, it does not lie in Scotland.

If we want to establish an economy built on common ownership, popular accountability and radically different power relations, we need to recognise that it will require large-scale intervention through the City of London and the British state. Giving up our democratic right to elect Members of Parliament (MPs) is unhelpful, to say the least.

The radical changes that working people and pensioners are crying out for not only in Scotland but across Britain will not be won if we wilfully ignore the balance of economic forces we face.

The big business, neoliberal perspective of the SNP also matters in respect of the new constitution, since once established, constitutions are not usually changed without a two-thirds majority. Making progressive change would also require the existence of a significant left movement, which currently does not exist – as evidenced by recent election results. The referendum itself and the process of negotiating national debts and assets is likely to strengthen nationalist as against left or class attitudes. And the Scottish left would then have to contend with the whole weight of the new national establishment and a big business owned press.

The White Paper is a far cry from the demands of the 1970s and '80s, when the balance of forces shifted significantly in favour of the left, driven by the Upper Clyde Shipbuilders (UCS), the Liverpool dockers and the miners.

In 1971, the UCS work-in demonstrated that Scotland's economy was not within its control. The STUC called for a Scottish Parliament – a 'workers' parliament' with real powers to act in the interests of working people.

The progressive movement pulled the Labour Party to the left so much that it went into the 1974 election calling for a 'fundamental and irreversible shift in the balance of power and wealth in favour of working people and their families.' The Labour Government later gave approval for a referendum on a Scottish Parliament in 1979 when a majority voted in favour, but it failed to meet the required minimum of 40 per cent of the electorate voting YES. This led to the SNP withdrawing its support for the Labour Government in Westminster, triggering a General Election and the return of the Tories, led by Margaret Thatcher.

A favourable balance of class forces was also built at the turn of the 20th century and can be seen in the history of pension provision. Before the Old Age Pensions Act was passed in 1908, older people who could no longer work depended on Poor Law charity to survive. It took ten years of the most rigorous British-wide campaigning led by trade unionists and social reformers to win the older people's right to a pension that would end the fear of dying in the workhouse.

The 1908 Pensions Act established the principle that the state had a responsibility to look after people in their older years. It can be seen as a progressive piece of social policy that would eventually lay the foundations for the creation of the welfare state in the 1940s by the post-war Labour Government.

In 1975, when there was an economic crisis and the Labour Government had a Parliamentary majority in single figures, the best pension provision ever was established. The 1975 Social Security Act recognised that the state pension was too low, women were poorer than men and that low paid and part-time workers always lost out when occupational pension schemes were established. The Act linked pensions to earnings or prices, depending on which rose faster, and established the State Earnings Related Pension scheme (SERPS) for all those not in an occupational scheme. It was quite an achievement and gave respect and hope to older people.

In the early months of the first Thatcher Government, Tory Chancellor Geoffrey Howe ended the link to earnings. John Major, then a junior Social Security Minister, spent much of 1986 piloting a social security bill through Parliament that seriously eroded SERPS. They said SERPS was 'unrealistic' and 'unsustainable' because life expectancy was rising – elderly people were living too long.

In its place came the personal portable pension scheme. What a gift for the private insurance industry, which had lobbied hard in favour of the change. The gross mis-selling of pensions led to scandals galore and eventually repayment to some victims of the private pension sharks.

Pensioners who hoped for a living state pension under the New Labour Government of Tony Blair were disappointed when it extended means testing through the introduction of The Pension Credit, raised the state pension age, and further developed the role of the private pensions industry via Personal Accounts – the same private industry that mis-sold personal pensions in the 1980s.

Con/Dem Chancellor George Osborne published his Autumn Statement on 5 December 2013. The pensioners of today will continue to have to access the means tested pension credit system. However, the Government will introduce a single-tier pension for people retiring after April 2017. This will be set just above the level of the pension credit, but that is still way below the official poverty level. The Government will accelerate the rise in the state pension age (ultimately rising to 70 in about 40 years) in line with alleged life expectancy. The treasury estimates this change will save the state up to £400 billion over the next half century. An independent review will assess likely lifespans every five years and will issue its first report after the 2015 election.

An independent Scottish Government will match George Osborne's statement in relation to pensions. However, there is one small difference, and it is this: 'Pensioners will receive a single-tier pension of £160 per week. That's £1.10 a week higher than the rate currently expected for the UK.' This sum is still below the official poverty level. This hardly resonates with an associated article in *YES for Independence* (Issue 2), which states: 'Everyone wants the security of a decent pension – and with independence, we'll make it happen.'

Clearly, independence will not end pensioner poverty. The current arrangements are heavily weighted towards the needs of the private pensions industry and this will continue to be the case. We are expected to take individual responsibility for taking out a private pension with minimal state backup. Struggling desperately to make ends meet makes individual saving for retirement an impossibility for millions of low paid people – especially women, who still experience income inequality. Poverty wages lead to poverty pensions for both men and women.

If this strategy is not changed, then the consequences for future generations of working people will be dire.

Britain nowadays is governed by thousands of directives (laws) issued by the EU that cannot be changed by Parliament at Westminster. This EU domination deprives the peoples of Britain of their rights to elect governments in this country that are intent on defending past gains or making real changes in favour of those who work for a living and pensioners. In truth, if political parties advocate membership of the EU, their policies cannot but be broadly the same and in favour of big business.

Services such as BT, energy, railways, the Post Office and parts of the welfare state, including pensions, have been privatised in line with EU competitive rules and the claim that private companies 'respond more efficiently to the market' – higher prices and misery for consumers and higher profits and wealth for owners.

In 2000, the European Round Table of Industrialists (ERT) produced the report 'European Pensions: An Appeal for Reform', which urged the EU to order member states to lift retirement ages, stop early retirement and encourage individuals to save for their retirement through private pension schemes.

By 2003, the EU issued a new Directive 2003/41/EC to force pension funds to comply with the internal Market principles of free movement of capital. (2014 and we are being advised to shop around for 'best value' annuities.)

Consider this. Although Britain is the sixth richest economy in the world, the Welfare State and its pension reforms are being destroyed to avoid government over-spending on limits imposed by the 'troika' – the unelected EU Commission, the unelected European Central Bank and the unelected US led International Monetary Fund through the EU Growth and Stability Pact.

The fact that pensioners in many other EU countries enjoy higher pensions owes more to their internal political struggles than to the EU itself. Affording pensions is not a matter of economics. It is a matter of politics.

In conclusion, the Thatcher Years have continued in substance through Blair, Cameron, and in Scotland by Alex Salmond. The common factor that binds them together is the EU. It follows therefore that the political breakup of the UK would not break up the British economy. Territorial separation would not weaken the grip of finance capital and its state institutions. The challenge before us – economic and social – will not be solved by independence or nationalism.

The rights that we have acquired are proof of the commitment and sacrifice made in working-class struggle through history. The revoking of a right, be it the welfare state/state pensions, or the right to self-determination in the form of a parliament – signals an unprecedented change in the balance of power. For the SNP to even be able to make the current proposal for Scottish independence shows that the force and influence of big business neoliberalism is on the rise, while that of the trade union and labour movement is seen to be on the wane.

But history shows that it is to the trade union and labour movement, working with others within legislatures, workplaces and communities that we must turn for a way out of the current economic crisis and progress towards equality, justice and socialism.

The labour movement alternative is urgently required. We need to re-establish the early promise of the Scottish Parliament and further develop its democratic powers. And at UK level, we need an overall redistribution of power and wealth from rich to poor and particularly from the City of London to the rest of the UK, thus bringing about the further democratisation of the UK state in the interests of working people throughout these islands.

The logic of this contribution calls for a 'no' vote in the upcoming referendum.

ELINOR MCKENZIE is a retired Further Education Lecturer. She is an active and 'hands-on' grandmother and great-gran. Currently an Executive Committee member of the Scottish Pensioners' Forum with a special interest in pensions and equality for women, she was formerly President of the EIS Further Education Section, Joint Secretary Scottish CND, and Chairperson Scottish Coalition for Justice Not War. She was the Communist Party candidate for a Glasgow constituency in the parliamentary elections to Westminster and to Holyrood in 2005 and 2007 respectively.

CHAPTER 11

A Scottish Asian Woman looks at Independence

SHABANA NAZ

1972 WAS THE year my father first stepped on to the tarmac of London Heathrow Airport direct from Islamabad. That same summer, the world was gripped by the tragic events unfolding at the Munich Olympics. Thirty years later, the world was equally gripped by the London Olympic Games. This time, however, it was the sheer celebration of life that kept everyone on the edge of their seats. It was the motto to 'Inspire a Generation' that particularly moved me and indeed the sentiment inspired me to start a new magazine for a new generation of Scottish Asians called *ID*.

Much has changed for the Scottish Asian since my father first drove up the M6 to Scotland. This first generation worked tirelessly to make a life, not just for themselves, but also for the family they left behind in their homeland. Whilst this issue is no longer a burden on the second and third generation of Scottish Asians today, our modern, fast-paced world presents a whole host of other issues, such as their integration and acceptance within the wider community. This has given rise to an identity crisis, questioning whether we are truly Scottish or truly Asian. It was my intention with *ID* to try to bridge the gap between the old and the new, by celebrating both the Scottish and Asian cultures and raising the issues which are most prevalent in the lives of the new cross-cultured generation.

However, one thing the first migrants realised, and the thought remains the same even today, is that we were able to be free to choose where we laid our foundations and made our home. Whether it was Land's End or John o' Groats, we had the freedom to live where we wanted and we were welcomed with open arms.

The question of Scottish independence, however, has made not just myself, but my entire family think about the consequences of having a new country. Many questions have come to mind and it makes me wonder about my life, possibly living in an independent state. So what will happen to Scotland? What will happen to us 'British' (albeit still very much Scottish) people? And can we survive as an independent nation? No matter how hard I look for positive answers, and with all the strategic and persuasive marketing from the pro-independence camp, I am not totally convinced becoming independent will be a good thing. Even more worrying is the thought of the effect such a step will have on us migrants.

I talk about migration because I know this is a question in the minds of many people, in particular the South Asian community in Scotland, who have many extended family members living in England, Wales and Northern Ireland.

I have a niece who is a doctor in Sheffield. She has just become a mother for the first time, and due to work commitments, we have to help her as much as possible. At the moment we can travel back and forth as soon as she is required at the hospital and juggle around her shift schedule. But after 18 September, will we be able to be there for her as much without having to deal with possible border controls, currency issues, fuel prices (in terms of travel costs on the train, buses and car)? This is just one example of what I fear may be a serious consideration point when I make my final decision about which cause I will be voting for.

At the moment, we enjoy freedom of movement. We are able to travel all over the UK without facing issues such as border controls, visa, currency differences, to name just a few. In this uncertain time and difficult financial climate, I feel the last thing I should have to worry about is my future in this country. Right now, as we are, we are reaping the benefits of being not only economically safe, but we have the safety of a great National Health Service, welfare system, excellent educational system, to name just a few. Even currently being a part of the UK has not meant we do not have a say in how our country is run. The Scottish Parliament has allowed Scotland to make its own mark and carve an identity of its own, so the question in my mind is – what do we not have at the moment that we will gain if we become an independent state?

Most of us mortgage payers struggle to not only keep up with the repayments, but also everyday bills. What will the impact on our mortgage interest rates be if we become a separate nation? One thing is clear. Everything that we benefit from today is likely not to be the same after 18 September. Another thing that is unequivocally clear is that if it happens, there is no going back. And this is probably the scariest thought to me.

A dream of independence is nice, but only if there truly is something better waiting for us. With possibly having to get a new passport, new currency and losing our place in the EU, it will be akin to travelling back in time to the dark ages. We have a say in how Scotland is run, so can we ask for anything more without losing everything we currently have?

Another issue that worries me is the difference in job opportunities. Many of my friends have managed to get a good position in companies in England. However, they are travelling home every so often to family. Restrictions which are likely to come into place if Scotland becomes independent will mean those who are trying to make a living may not be able to see their family so easily, and will be isolated from home, having to face rules and regulations before coming home to visit. With us remaining a part of the UK, however, it also allows us to continue bene-fitting from the job opportunities we have just now, and with those restrictions, Scotland is likely to face a jobs crisis as well as a lack of opportunity to progress.

As someone who has a family history of health issues, I know I can benefit from the country's NHS system, but the Scottish Parliament also has the right to make its own decisions about the healthcare we receive here too. Even though Scotland has a fabulous setup of its own in terms of its healthcare, we may not be able to benefit from healthcare anywhere else in the UK. So if I am visiting my niece in Sheffield, and fall ill, I may not be able to benefit from the NHS help I can here.

As a strong member of the EU and as the UK as a whole, no one can deny that the UK is a force to be reckoned with throughout the world. Scotland on its own will not have that impact and influence, leaving us in a weaker position and possibly without a voice in Europe. I don't want to be just a small dot on the world map, a likelihood of independence.

Scotland is also renowned to have some of the best universities in the UK, educating some of the world's best scientists and inventors. However, a great deal of funding for these great institutions is backed by the rest of the UK. Independent Scotland will pose a grave threat to this and the impact Scotland has on the UK currently will lessen, perhaps even diminish. I don't want my children to have fewer opportunities in terms of the educational system or have to face many coinciding issues if they have to move away to be able to get the level of education they want.

Our sterling allows us to be able to have lower interest rates. This is most likely to not be the case if we have to work with a brand new currency, still to be established, recognised, valued throughout the world – the list can go on.

In my mind, the argument can go on, but time is of the essence. With just a few months left, we are heading towards the biggest decision of a lifetime, one that could potentially change life in Scotland forever. I am not willing to live with a question mark over my life. When we clench our hand, we make a fist. That fist is more powerful than our individual fingers. Scotland, England, Ireland and Wales are stronger together because we become that fist. Our unity is our strength, and that is something we cannot compromise. Scotland must stay together. We have too much to lose.

SHABANA NAZ is the co-founder of the first and only ever full-time Asian radio station, leading on to begin a career in print media. She founded *Awaz Newspaper* in 2002, until she felt it was time to do something new. It was this urge for something different that made her co-found and begin the *ID* Magazine. This is the first of its kind in Scotland, aiming to serve a gap in the market for an Asian lifestyle magazine. Nineteen months later, it has made a home for itself on the coffee tables of an estimated 50,000 readers throughout Greater Glasgow.

CHAPTER 12

Four Trees Standing Together

FIONA O'DONNELL MP

WHEN I WAS asked to contribute to this publication, I was told that it should be a personal piece. That is easy. For me, the issues around the independence debate are intensely personal in terms of my history, my family, my life experiences and my values.

I am someone who believes in the redistribution of wealth, that those who have most should contribute more to the benefit of those who have less. That is a debate that is framed around our sense of community, and for me that community extends beyond the borders of Scotland. I find it deeply disappointing that so much of the debate is framed in terms of whether we will be worse or better off in an independent Scotland. I also care about whether the people I feel connected to in the rest of the UK will be better or worse off. We Scots may have lost out on some of the wealth from oil exploration because we have shared that, not only with our fellow Brits, but within the EU and in tackling poverty in developing countries. That is something I am proud of. I think that is a rich stream that runs through Scottish society, that we care about the wellbeing of others. We may be a small nation, but we have big hearts.

It is widely acknowledged that economic factors are central to most people's thinking on the independence referendum. Figures are set out by both sides of the argument that at times appear to contradict each other. Speaking to voters all across my constituency I find that many reply that they do not feel qualified to weigh up this conflicting evidence and come to a conclusion. There is an awareness, particularly among older people, that the decision they make will live on well beyond their life span and it will be future generations who will judge whether we made the right decision on 18 September.

I would not disagree that the potential economic impact of independence is crucial, perhaps even decisive, to the outcome of the debate. However, I do believe that other factors will also play an important part as Scots make up their minds on how to vote. In particular, I think it is inevitable that personal experiences and emotional issues, such as family ties, will feature prominently in people's deliberations.

One of my great political heroes, the late Tony Benn, spoke in emotional terms about Scottish independence a couple of years ago. He said,

> If Scotland wants to be independent they have the absolute right to do so. But I think nationalism is a mistake. And I am half Scots and feel it would divide me in half with a knife. The thought that my mother would suddenly be a foreigner would upset me very much.

I can understand his sentiments and, for me, the personal and emotional side of the debate is intensely important. The 'social union' has always been very much a reality for my family. My mother, who was from Cornwall originally, met my Irish father in The Gorbals in Glasgow. They emigrated to Canada, where I was born, before returning to live in the Highlands, where I grew up.

I have four children, three of whom were born in England. My daughter, three sons and I value the experience of living in other parts of the United Kingdom. I often found as our family moved around England following work opportunities that I gravitated towards other Scots. However, I always made English friends with whom I found I had just as much in common. It was a positive decision to return home to Scotland as the eldest entered secondary education. So for my family, with two of my sons now living and working in England, though at times their work as musicians means that they work in Scotland too given the strong cultural ties between different parts of the UK, Scotland separating from the rest of the UK in terms of its political, economic and social ties, would also mean degrees of separation for our family.

My third son lives in another part of the EU and with the joyous arrival of a son to him and his Swedish partner also came the complexities of my grandson's nationality. I would not want that for any future grandchildren born in England. Not because it is an intolerable burden or because I cannot see the many advantages for a grandson with triple nationality. I rail against this future for any grandchildren born in England because I do not want them to be born in a foreign country.

That belief has grown in me as a result of my own parentage, my experience of living in England and my many family and friendship connections in all parts of the UK.

In understanding myself and explaining to others why I do not support independence, my own family's history is part of my conviction. But I knew this somewhere within me before I was aware of my family history and before I had lived the greater part of my life.

I have known since my early years that I was not a nationalist. I remember a conversation on the Fort William Primary School minibus. Another girl took out a sweetie paper, tore it in half, and explained to me that this was what happened to Scotland's wealth as a consequence of our union with the rest of the UK. I acknowledge that the nationalist argument has moved on from sweetie papers, and the SNP's White Paper has considerably more substance – who can claim that there is no room for generosity in this debate! For me no matter how many economic and social arguments are advanced by the SNP and the wider YES campaign, I cannot get past the fact that Scotland, as part of the UK, is better placed to do good here at home and around the world.

It feels to me that this is somehow more important than a narrowly defined national identity, based on a fixed notion of what it means to be Scottish. It is this powerful, if at times slightly intangible sense of Britishness, which I think remains important to many other Scots, particularly the millions who have family living in other parts of the UK. I see our family of nations like four trees standing together. Each has its own identity, but under the surface our roots are entangled. To try and separate one from the others would damage all.

Solidarity with working-class communities in other parts of the UK, and the desire to do good both here in the UK and abroad, is also of crucial importance to my own view of Scotland's place in the world. I lived in different parts of England, including Newcastle, Banbury and Cheltenham for a number of years. I tire of the suggestion that people there are different in their attitudes or outlook to Scots, a contention which is certainly not borne out by my own experience.

Of course, parts of the south of England are more affluent and people in those areas tend to be more inclined to vote Tory than here in Scotland or the north of England. However, it is important to remember that even in 2010, when Labour suffered one of its heaviest electoral defeats, more than 1.6 million people still voted for the party across the south and east of England.

Opinion surveys also suggest that there is actually not nearly as much difference in the political and social outlook north and south of the border as some would have us believe. 'What England Wants?', a paper published last year by Professor John Curtice of Edinburgh University, explored this issue using the results of the British and Scottish Social Attitude surveys. It found Scottish attitudes to be only marginally more 'social democratic' than those of the English:

> When it comes to levels of concern about inequality, the two countries often look rather similar indeed. For example, the 61 per cent of people in Scotland who think that 'there is one law for the rich and one for the poor' is fully matched by the 63 per cent of people in England who take the same view.

This confirms my long-held view that working-class Scots in the central belt have far more in common with those from similar backgrounds in Birmingham, Bristol or Brighton than big landowners in other parts of Scotland. As someone with deeply held progressive political values, which I know some on the YES side share, we do not advance those in the cause of the greatest good for the many by choosing the division of nationalism over solidarity with people in similar circumstances who just happen to live a couple of hundred miles down the road.

Proud to take part in a local commemoration of the miners' strike in Prestonpans Labour Club, I recalled this was where our local party, spurred on by my predecessor and great supporter of home rule, John P. Mackintosh, passed the first motion to go to our conference calling for a Scottish Parliament. The two traditions sit comfortably together. When we face the same struggles and injustices in different parts of the UK, we are better able to fight the good fight when we stand shoulder to shoulder. Mackintosh, who was so instrumental in urging the Labour Party to embrace the concept of devolution, once said:

> People in Scotland want a degree of government for themselves. It is not beyond the wit of man to devise the institution to meet those demands.

After the Labour victory in 1997, the UK Parliament delivered that institution and the Scottish Parliament has been a great success. Rather than ripping up the current arrangements I want to see people in Scotland working together with our friends and neighbours in the rest of the UK to make devolution even more effective. I have been deeply moved by the number of Labour MPs from England and Wales who have spoken about how important it is to our shared endeavour that Scotland remains part of the UK. Dennis Skinner has told me he makes the case everywhere he goes. He and others want to engage in this debate and are keeping the pressure on we Scots to do more.

My opposition to Scottish independence has grown stronger in my present job as the Scottish Labour Member of Parliament for East Lothian. I have been privileged to be a member of the House of Commons' International Development Committee for some time now. It has afforded me the opportunity to see firsthand the incredible difference that the UK's investment in aid and development makes around the globe. This is something I feel immense pride in. The fact that so much of the work done by UK Aid is delivered by staff here in Scotland makes it even better.

This desire to do good abroad that has been shown by successive UK governments undermines the SNP's narrative that everything about Westminster and the UK is bad. While I would be the first to admit that we can always do more, and have concerns about some of the decisions that have been made by the Coalition Government, the fact is that the UK has made a huge and lasting difference to the lives of millions of the world's poorest people.

I am sure that an independent Scotland would be committed to doing as much as it could to assist people in the developing world. The harsh reality is, however, that it would be impossible to replicate the impact and reach of the UK's current aid and development programme, no matter whether the will to try and do good is there, or not. I think it is illuminating that the SNP's White Paper contains just two pages on international development policy, much of which is dedicated to outlining how an independent Scotland would seek to continue working closely with the rest of the UK. When we are asked what a NO vote will mean for Scotland, I hope that it will mean that we talk less about drawing powers to Holyrood and more about devolving power from there to councils and communities.

I will be spending as much time as I can in the run up to the referendum in September talking to people about why I believe they should vote No. I would rather be spending all that time talking to them about why we need to get rid of this Coalition Government. But I will make the argument for Scotland to remain within the UK with all the energy, reason and passion I can muster, because I know that if on 18 September Scotland votes to leave the UK I will be devastated, and I will feel that on a very personal level.

FIONA O'DONNELL has been the Member of Parliament for East Lothian since 6 May 2010. Upon being elected to Parliament, she served as a member of the Scottish Affairs Select Committee and as Parliamentary Private Secretary to the then Shadow Secretary of State for Health, the Rt Hon John Healey MP. From October 2011 to June 2012, she served as Shadow Minister for the Natural Environment and Fisheries. In 2012 she joined Parliament's International Development Committee. She is also currently a member of the Commons' Committees on Standards and Privileges.

CHAPTER 13

It's Not Just a Cross on a Piece of Paper

KARA ROSS

UNTIL RECENTLY, I had never really thought about the reasons I was voting NO in the fast approaching referendum. I had come up with countless reasons during arguments with my friends, most of which revolve around an inherent distrust of the Scottish National Party and of nationalism itself. However, realising in the past few months that it was perhaps time to consider something more substantial, I began to consider exactly what my feelings towards the debate were. At first my findings were somewhat surprising. I thought first about why other people I knew were so ardent in their YES – going beyond the pale of North Sea oil. Moving away from a petty debate about how many hundreds of pounds richer each of us would be either way, I tried to think about the bigger ideas steering many people towards the prospect of an independent Scotland. I considered the fact that some were voting YES out of a regard for social democracy; the belief that only once we cast off the shackles of Westminster will we catch a glimpse of the enlightened, just society so many in Scotland (supposedly) desire is not a rare one. People want rid of the outdated institutions and elitist system that fails to serve a vast section of the population. Is it not my desire to live in a country of equality? Am I not increasingly disillusioned by the ability or the inclination of those who run our country to deliver this? Why (oh, why) then, am I voting NO?

The truth is I don't disagree with the facts that many nationalists cite as their motives. The problem is perhaps that I am more pessimistic than them. Although some would be all too happy to fatten their campaign on my morose negativity, it is my belief that some sense of reality must be upheld in this debate. Unfortunately, after much due consideration, I have come to the conclusion that while I would love to see our nation ignite into a Scandinavian beacon of social reform, I don't see voting YES as a means to this end.

It seems to me that in many ways the referendum is a copout. The easy option. With all the fervour in the world, the problems facing our nation cannot, and will not, be swept over the border at the sweet moment of fond farewell. The parallels in Scottish and British society run too deep for us to be rid of them by simply turning our back on our neighbours and although the real issues that prevent any change in our nation are most obviously discerned in Westminster, it is naïve to believe that they end there. If we really reject the elitism of British politics that has left so many people disillusioned and disenfranchised, if we really wish to see a real departure from it, then that has to be something we're prepared to fight for. But apathy has struck a nation once ready to scream and shout for its cause. The ruling class must take account for many of the problems in our society and the student protests of 2010 have shown that it now may not be safe to protest in the same ways as people used to but we must accept, in part at least, the people at the top are able to get away with as much as they do because we let them. So my real worry is, if the YES vote succeeds and the kinds of changes the Scottish people seem to so ardently desire don't occur (and looking at the White Paper there is no reason to suggest they will), will people object? Or will those with the power to effect change be content in the knowledge that their taxes are low and lowering even whilst promised public spending remains in the same position?

It is also worth noting that in many respects the independence proposal is nowhere near as revolutionary as it's made out to be. If we truly believe that the union is holding us back then why aren't we proposing to get rid of its signature institutions? The Queen is to remain our head of state and our currency will be controlled by British banks. Apart from the obvious scruples about the affordability of the Scottish Government's pension plan, the idea that they will be administered within a new Scottish organisation but still protected under the UK Pension Protection Fund is a telling example of the lack of a clear vision for what independence will look like. This is not something we can do half-heartedly; for independence to work, we need a strong proposal and a definite break from the rest of the UK. Treading the paths of conjecture and hesitancy is simply not acceptable at this stage. We hold a somewhat privileged position in our country; represented in our own parliament and in one of the most internationally recognised governments in the world. To give up this potentially extremely powerful station we should be careful to make sure it is for something at the very least concrete.

Although nowadays we often hear that the UK is doomed, defunct and heading towards catastrophe, to say there is no hope with absolute certainty is ridiculous. The United Kingdom has huge potential but much of this lies in size and diversity. I don't particularly agree with the doomsday argument that Scottish independence will resemble the apocalypse, collapsing into an irreversible decline without the rest of the UK subsidising our national inadequacy, but I don't believe either that without the union a liberated Scotland will skip into the sunset. In the event of the YES vote reigning victorious both sides of the border will undoubtedly endure great financial upheaval and for many this may prove to be disastrous. The financial sense of remaining in the union is as clear as it was when Scotland joined in 1707. We go on and on about what makes Scotland and the Scottish people so unique but this is precisely why the union of our four small nations has such great potential to work. The diversity of our nations means that often while one country suffers in one area another will be able to support it; we are not only buoyed by our own successes but those of three other countries which surely indicates the potential our country has for prosperity and security.

My simple belief is that growth and change comes from working together. As we face huge global problems over the coming decades I cannot think that we will solve them by becoming more insular or inward looking and by turning our back on the union that is precisely what we are doing. YES, there are problems closer to home concerning British politics but these can be rectified and I believe the referendum can have positive effects in starting to tackle them. It has highlighted that many people, not only in Scotland but in Wales, Northern Ireland and even the north of England, feel ignored by Westminster which must be recognised as a problem. It has made many people who have become totally disengaged with politics think again about the problems facing our society and, more importantly, about alternatives. I have the small hope that come October 2014 we will see not a union divided but one whole, imbued with a people ready to question what is going on around them and perhaps even fight against it. I want to see change but I believe the changes most beneficial to us take more effort than a cross on a piece of paper.

KARA ROSS is 18 years old. She comes from Glasgow but is currently living in Edinburgh where she is in her first year studying French and English Literature. In her spare time, she plays netball and tries to read as much as she can, but mostly she watches far too much TV and drinks a lot of tea.

CHAPTER 14

SNP – Something Not Proven

CLLR KATE STEPHEN

WHEN I WAS growing up in the Highlands, I was aware of a lot of anti-English feeling. English people were buying up old crofts; either doing them up and moving in or using the croft houses for holiday homes. If they lived here, they were accused of changing the place by not speaking Gaelic and not understanding our ways. If they kept the place as a holiday home, they might face a 'go home' slogan in graffiti on their freshly whitewashed wall.

No one encouraged me to hate the English but no-one would have told me off if I said out loud that I did. Well, they were still going on about winning the World Cup and they were stealing our oil and so it was perfectly normal to dislike them. To 'be the nation again' was not just a line of my favourite song, it was a mission call.

So, what happened to change me from a Nationalist child to a Unionist adult? The answers are: the Battle of Culloden, borders and Bosnia. Let me explain.

I had thought of England as the enemy so it was discomforting to learn that a lot of the bad guys in our history were Scottish. I was horrified that Scottish people could behave so badly to each other: the clan warfare, the evictions during the clearances. And then came the brutal blow; my clan was on the wrong side at Culloden! I had always seen myself as a Jacobite, that in a different time it might have been me who rowed the Bonnie Prince over the sea to Skye. So this news came as a shock that made me reflect on the difference between who I thought I was, who I actually was, and what difference did it make anyway!

Over the years I've become quite interested in borders. It started off when I crossed the border to England. What an anti-climax! I expected it to look and feel different. In the 'us and them' scenario, it made me realise it was not always so easy to differentiate who was who. Travelling further afield, I noticed that people who live close to a border tend to assert their identity, based on which side of the border they're on. More so than people who live in central areas. In France, in the Ardennes region, the nearer you get to the border the more French flags start to appear. Driving nearby into Luxembourg, Germany and Belgium, many houses display flags in their windows to remind you which country you're in. One of my daughters boasted about going to Germany all by herself when she was eight years old. In reality, all this involved was her running across a footbridge over a river!

Most of our borders and the sides we find ourselves on could be described as accidents of fate, decided by historic power negotiations or royal gifts which might then determine language and religious practice as well as identity. People from villages and towns around the Scottish-English border have only in relatively recent history been able to have confidence in their nationality as before they shifted from one to the other, depending on which raids were successful.

Nowadays borders tend to be drawn to help the administration of public services. It determines who empties your bin, which hospital you get sent to and who you apply to for business support. The lack of consistency between various public agencies can be frustrating, confusing and costly. The frustration and costs are higher when the borders are at state or national scale.

But the nationalism within me was well and truly knocked into touch when I saw what was happening to the former Yugoslavia from 1992. Where neighbours and people who went to school together began to assert their differences more than their similarities. They then redefined who they were accordingly. They sought to separate from each other and ended up in a horrific war with mass rape and ethnic cleansing. I am obviously not saying that nationalism inevitably leads to this end but I recognise much in its language that dangerously points, and could ultimately lead, in that direction.

Current Scottish Nationalist rhetoric defines an 'us and them' mentality and bases accusations of inequality and injustice on these arbitrary and fictional differences. If it wasn't for 'them', we would be richer, stronger, fairer and so on when all along we are as much 'them' as they are. And they are redefining what it means to be Scottish; separate and superior. Dangerous stuff. It reminds me of the anti-English attitudes of my childhood.

It doesn't have to be this way. We can value our uniqueness and respect our differences in a way that helps us live at peace with each other. And by developing cultural, trade and legislative links we can embed mutual benefit and common understanding. And by working together, at various levels, we are stronger. The UK is an example of where this strength is so much more than its constituent parts. It is strength at a global level.

I wish the arguments around independence were based on practical considerations about the optimum scale for the efficient delivery of government services. I'd like to hear about where there might be efficiencies or greater effectiveness in doing things differently, at a smaller Scottish scale? But many indicators suggest a loss of efficiency and the costly setting up of smaller, separate bureaucratic infrastructures. There is an inconsistency between the prospect of this and the SNP-led direction of travel currently within Scotland towards centralisation. Where they have taken away our smaller, accountable structures to create a unitary, centrally based organisation with the promise that this is to save money.

It seems logical to think that some things would be lost and some things would be gained by separating and going it alone. But whenever there is any attempt to describe what will be lost, accusations of scaremongering are made and bland reassurances given. Bland reassurances are also given when the detail of what is to be gained is examined.

When I hear SNP speakers on the radio refer to the White Paper, saying that a particular question has been answered on page whatever, I quite often look up the page. I am dismayed by what I read. Because what I read is another bland reassurance with no detail. No answer.

The most recent example of this was on the topic of future research funding. Currently Scottish universities and research centres can apply to a wide range of UK research councils and charities. Because of their high quality proposals, Scottish Institutions receive over 13 per cent of UK Research Council funding (they would only receive eight per cent if it was decided on size). In research, success breeds success as capacity is built and maintained. A future independent Scotland would have to pay much more than its share in order to sustain current levels. Additional funding would be required to compensate for the charitable funding no longer available. The consequences of not doing so is the decline of research output, erosion of capacity and reputation, and a knock on deterioration in the quality of our universities. Decline breeds decline. There would be consequences for the wider economy as more of our young people would have to leave Scotland to get the specialised education they require to obtain professional jobs. In the Highlands we know that when the young people leave for education, they often stay away.

So where is the evidence of how my concerns will be addressed? I would want evidence that research funding would be a priority for the new independent Scotland but all the White Paper says is that the future would involve seeking to continue current arrangements and renegotiating a funding formula with Westminster. Keeping the status quo but paying more for it! Yet somehow promising more influence to boot! No mention of compensating for the loss of charitable grants. Ironically, the SNP are saying we are better together for research funding but they will close doors and add uncertainty and increased costs for an independent Scotland. Our senior academics are worried and have produced 'Excelling Together' with concerns about the loss of funding.

Despite all this, surprisingly, there must be, still, deep down, a Nationalist child in me. It is the part of me that swells with pride when I see the saltire waving in the wind. It is the part of me that boasts about Scotland being the best country in the world. And it is the longing I have to be here and remain here. Most revealing of all, it is the vain hope of sporting victory and matched with the notion that defeat can be tolerated – unless the victor is England. It is that child which responds to being told by a strong Scottish voice that 'we can do it, we can be a nation again!'

But the decision I am being asked to make on 18 September is too important, too serious and too permanent to be made by a childish heart. It requires mature consideration where I can objectively and dispassionately evaluate the pros and cons – like a canny Scot. For me, the case for independence has not been made and the bland reassurances are sounding ever emptier. For me, SNP stands for Something Not Proven.

KATE STEPHEN is a Liberal Democrat and an elected member of Highland Council. She is their Champion for Older People and Adults with Support Needs. Kate represents the Culloden and Ardersier Ward. She has been selected as the Liberal Democrat candidate for the Scottish Parliament constituency Skye, Lochaber and Badenoch. Her interest in getting involved in politics has grown from her paid and voluntary work in community development and community care. Kate is also a PhD student with the University of the Highlands and Islands. She is researching the role of technology in the motivation and adherence to exercise. She is interested in challenges around demographic change and rurality, especially in health services. Most of Kate's family come from the Isle of Skye but Kate was born in Dingwall in Ross-Shire. She has spent most of her life in the Highlands and Islands.

Remember Mary Barbour

The campaign to create a lasting memorial to a great Govan hero

What Mary Barbour did has become better known recently, because of interest in the First World War. When so many men were away at the Front, and workers were pouring into Glasgow desperate for housing, landlords thought the women would be a soft touch when they raised the rents. Mary Barbour wasn't having it. She organised the tenants' resistance, and when some were taken to court she led a huge march through the city. The government promptly passed a law restricting rents throughout Britain to pre-War levels.

Herald and Times Archive

Mary was also a campaigner for peace. In 1920 she became one of the first female councillors in Glasgow, and set about making life better for the families in the tenements. Pure milk free for schoolchildren. Public wash-houses. Child welfare centres where children could play. She organised the first birth control clinic in Scotland and a child welfare clinic.

Her life has already been commemorated in some ways – in the naming of the 'Mary Barbour suite' in the Pearce Institute in Govan, the collection of rent strike artefacts such as the rattle on show in the National Museum of Scotland and the film 'Red skirts on Clydeside'. The song 'Mrs Barbour's Army' by Alistair Hulett is about Mary Barbour's organisation of the 1915 rent strike. Mary Barbour was the subject of one of the 'Not Forgotten' series of documentaries on Channel 4 in 2007. Over 2011–2012 Sharon Thomas, a Glasgow-based artist, created a project to document and honour Mary gathering together information and images used in an artwork for the Glasgow Women's Library.

Direct and forthright, Mary Barbour was a strong, energetic and convincing campaigner who helped to make the world a different place from the one that was in war-torn crisis in 1915.

Read more about her, and the campaign to make these events more widely known, on the Remember Mary Barbour website. **http://remembermarybarbour.wordpress.com/**

The authors of the essays published in this book have asked that all royalties from the sale of this book go to the Remember Mary Barbour fund, which aims to have a statue erected at Govan Cross, Glasgow, in time for the centenary of the Rent Strike in November 2015.

Scotland's Referendum: A Guide for Voters

Jamie Maxwell & David Torrance
ISBN 978-1-910021-54-5 PBK £5.99

On 18 September 2014, everyone in Scotland aged 16 or over will be asked the question: 'Should Scotland Be An Independent Country?'

As the referendum approaches, the debates over whether or not Scotland should be an independent country are becoming more heated. This guide, produced by respected Scottish journalists and authors, Jamie Maxwell and David Torrance, covers everything you need to know in advance of deciding which way to vote.

Maxwell and Torrance summarise the main arguments for and against before delving into the central issues at the heart of the debate, including economics, welfare and pensions, defence and foreign affairs, and culture and national identity.

They outline the way that Scotland is currently governed and review where the parties stand on the debate before concluding with speculative

chapters on what happens after the vote, whether YES or NO. The referendum on 18 September 2014 is the most significant democratic event in Scotland's history. Get engaged. Be informed. Whatever you do, don't NOT vote!

Britain Rebooted: Scotland in a Federal Union

David Torrance
ISBN: 978-1-910021-11-8 £7.99 PBK

Would federalism work in the UK?

Wouldn't England dominate a British federation?

How would powers be distributed between federal and Home Nation level? What about the House of Lords?

In the run up to the historic referendum on Scottish independence there has been a plethora of tracts, articles and books arguing for and against, but there remains a gap in the literature: the case for Scotland becoming part of a 'rebooted' federal Union. It is an old, usually Liberal, dream, but one still worth fighting for.

It is often assumed that federalism is somehow 'alien' to the Scottish and British constitutional tradition but in this short book journalist David Torrance argues that not only has the UK already become a quasi-federal state but that formal federation is the best way of squaring the competing demands of Nationalists and Unionists.

He also uses Scotland's place within a federal UK to examine other potential reforms with a view to tackling ever-increasing inequality across the British Isles and create a more equal, successful and constitutionally coherent country.

Scotland: A Suitable Case for Treatment
Tom Brown and Henry McLeish
ISBN: 978-1-906307-69-1 PBK £9.99

 Joining forces again to attack the political establishment, Tom Brown and Henry McLeish embark on a comprehensive examination of the ailments ravaging Scotland and the Union. The diagnosis? That the Scots are a schizophrenic people in crisis whose internal tumult has been writ large on recent British politics. What is called for is radical change, for a 'new politics', for a more confident nation that can bury the hatchet with England and stand alone as a leader in a global world.

Blossom: What Scotland Needs to Flourish
Lesley Riddoch
ISBN: 978-1-908373-69-4 PBK £11.99

 Weeding out vital components of Scottish identity from decades of political and social tangle is no mean task, but it's one journalist Lesley Riddoch has undertaken.

Dispensing with the tired, yo-yoing jousts over fiscal commissions, devo something-or-other and EU in-or-out, Blossom pinpoints both the buds of growth and the blight that's holding Scotland back. Drawing from its people and history, as well as the experience of the Nordic countries and the author's own passionate and outspoken perspective, this is a plain-speaking but incisive call to restore equality and control to local communities and let Scotland flourish.

Not so much an intervention in the independence debate as a heartfelt manifesto for a better democracy.
THE SCOTSMAN

World in Chains
The Impact of Nuclear Weapons and Militarisation from a UK Perspective
Edited by Angie Zelter
ISBN 978-1-910021-03-3 PBK £12.99

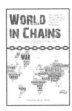

World in Chains is a collection of essays from well-reputed experts, all of which deliver engaging and analytical critiques of nuclear warfare.

In the past I have often wondered why obviously unethical or inhumane horrors were able to take place, what people were doing at the time to prevent them or what kind of resistance was happening, how many people knew and tried to stop the genocide, slavery, poverty and pollution… I want those who come after my generation to know that, yes, we do know of the dangers of nuclear war, of climate chaos, of environmental destruction. This book will show you that there were many people working to change the structures that keep our world in chains. ANGIE ZELTER

It is simply very hard to read, or think, about oneself and all of one's loved ones – all of the people one knows – strangers, everyone… being evaporated, or burned alive, being poisoned, blinded, tormented, genetically altered, starved, deprived of all they own and so forth… Thinking about nuclear weapons is just hard.
A. L. KENNEDY

[Angie Zelter] is committed to working to prevent nuclear mass murder, and by her own personal example and through her organizational skills, she has inspired and empowered many people.
MAIREAD CORRIGAN MAGUIRE (1976 Nobel Peace Prize Winner)

Small Nations in a Big World
Michael Keating and Malcolm Harvey
ISBN: 978-1-910021-20-0 PBK £9.99

Small northern European nations have been a major point of reference in the Scottish independence debate. For nationalists, they have been an 'arc of prosperity' while in the aftermath of the financial crash, unionists lampooned the 'arc of insolvency'. Both characterisations are equally misleading. Small nations can do well in the global marketplace, yet they face the world in very different ways. Some accept market logic and take the 'low road' of low wages, low taxes and light regulation, with a correspondingly low level of public services. Others take the 'high road' of social investment, which entails a larger public sector and higher taxes. Such a strategy requires innovative government, flexibility and social partnership.

Keating and Harvey compare the experience of the Nordic and Baltic states and Ireland, which have taken very different roads and ask what lessons can be learnt for Scotland. They conclude that an independent nation is possible but that hard choices would need to be taken.

Details of these and other books published by Luath Press can be found at:
www.luath.co.uk

Luath Press Limited
committed to publishing well written books worth reading

LUATH PRESS takes its name from Robert Burns, whose little collie Luath (*Gael.*, swift or nimble) tripped up Jean Armour at a wedding and gave him the chance to speak to the woman who was to be his wife and the abiding love of his life. Burns called one of 'The Twa Dogs' Luath after Cuchullin's hunting dog in Ossian's *Fingal*. Luath Press was established in 1981 in the heart of Burns country, and now resides a few steps up the road from Burns' first lodgings on Edinburgh's Royal Mile.
Luath offers you distinctive writing with a hint of unexpected pleasures.

Most bookshops in the UK, the US, Canada, Australia, New Zealand and parts of Europe either carry our books in stock or can order them for you. To order direct from us, please send a £sterling cheque, postal order, international money order or your credit card details (number, address of cardholder and expiry date) to us at the address below. Please add post and packing as follows: UK – £1.00 per delivery address; overseas surface mail – £2.50 per delivery address; overseas airmail – £3.50 for the first book to each delivery address, plus £1.00 for each additional book by airmail to the same address. If your order is a gift, we will happily enclose your card or message at no extra charge.

Luath Press Limited
543/2 Castlehill
The Royal Mile
Edinburgh EH1 2ND
Scotland
Telephone: 0131 225 4326 (24 hours)
Fax: 0131 225 4324
email: sales@luath.co.uk
Website: www.luath.co.uk